Writing Themes
About Literature

PRENTICE-HALL INTERNATIONAL, INC., LONDON
PRENTICE-HALL OF AUSTRALIA, PTY., LTD., SYDNEY
PRENTICE-HALL OF CANADA, LTD., TORONTO
PRENTICE-HALL OF INDIA (PRIVATE) LTD., NEW DELHI
PRENTICE-HALL OF JAPAN, INC., TOKYO
PRENTICE-HALL DE MEXICO, S.A., MEXICO CITY

Writing Themes

About Literature

Edgar V. Roberts

Hunter College

PRENTICE-HALL, INC.

Englewood Cliffs, N.J.

Fourth printing. . . . . April, 1965

Printed in the United States of America
[97070–C]

for Nanette

Acknowledgments

I should like to thank Professor Robert Daniel of Kenyon College, who read this entire book in manuscript. His patience and care, his many suggestions for improvement, his corrections of errors, and his stylistic comments have been invaluable. To my students at Hunter College in the Bronx, on whom I have tested each chapter, I express my thanks. Without them and their patience in tolerating early drafts, this book could not have existed. Finally I should like to thank my wife, who not only read, corrected, and improved the manuscript, but assisted in preparing it for the press.

Table of Contents

To the Instructor

THIS book provides a fresh and interesting approach to the writing of themes on literary topics. Each assignment is about a phase of literary study which is usually considered in literature and composition courses. The book is different from handbooks, rhetorics, textbooks on poetry and prose, and collections of critical essays, because it concentrates upon literary problems *as* they bear upon the writing of themes. I have tried to keep in focus the needs of the student with a difficult assignment on a work of literature, and I have emphasized how the assignment may be treated within the confines of a theme. This approach is new; it has the virtue of making the theoretical discussion of a technique of literary criticism immediately vital to the student. If he can see a literary problem in the light of his necessity to write about it, he is more likely to learn his lesson well. The book might be called a rhetoric of practical criticism for students.

Students need guidance before they write a theme about literature. It is a common complaint among teachers that papers on literary topics written by their students are not really to the point. The reason is simple: the majority of students asked to "analyze the structure of X play, or Y poem, or Z short story" do not really understand what structure is or how to go about analyzing it. Students asked to discuss "point of view in X literary work" are similarly handicapped, and so on through most of the themes they write about literature. Under these conditions, instructors either waste valuable time explaining theme assignments, or else continue to receive inadequate student writing about literature. This book is offered as a solution. It aims to free instructors from the drudgery and lost time of making assignments, and to help students by explaining and illustrating many approaches to literary technique in order to provide a sound basis for analysis. The practical aim of the book is to aid students in improving their reading and writing skills.

Many other books have been published with these ends in view, but

I have not found them satisfactory. They present works by distinguished literary critics like I. A. Richards and Virginia Woolf, dealing with subjects like "Badness in Poetry" and "The Novels of Thomas Hardy." Presumably, after reading these masters, the student is expected to imitate them.

I believe that this approach is not practical for the college classroom. The examples from the professional critics and scholar-teachers may deal with many literary techniques, but their main concern is not to assist the student who has a composition to write. Examples of this sort are anywhere from five to twenty times longer than the composition expected from the student; they are usually subtle and sophisticated, referring with easy familiarity to writers unknown to the student; the technical approaches are often either too complex or too advanced for the student's use. The result is that he is confused, not helped. At his age he cannot be expected to write as the critics do; nor can he be expected to receive more than limited benefit from the critics. He needs clear directions and short examples which are not only in accord with his understanding but similar to the theme he is expected to write. The assignments in this book fit this need. They have all been worked out in the classroom, and have demonstrably helped students improve their themes about literature.

While the assignments can stand alone, you may wish to use them as bases for discussions before assignments are due, or as supplements to the discussions. Of course, the assignments may be modified if you so desire. In their present form, however, they can assist you immeasurably in the assigning of themes. Too frequently, when assignments are made orally, students lose important directions; there is many a slip between your lip and the student's notebook. This book is therefore designed to make assignments clear and unequivocal, so that no questions should arise late on the night before an assignment is due.

Each chapter is devoted to the consideration of a separate literary approach that creates a problem in composition. There is first a discussion of the problems caused by the particular assignment, and second a sample theme that should be within the scope of the undergraduate. The discussions are always focused upon critical techniques as they bear upon writing assigned to students. The sample themes show how a student might handle the various assignments. While many students will follow the patterns closely, many others will wish to adapt the discussions and samples to their own needs. The result in either case should be superior student writing.

The samples have been conceived and written in the belief that the word *imitation* does not need to be preceded by words like *slavish* or *mere*. Much bad undergraduate writing results from uncertainty about what is expected in the way of imitation. While the student seeks a *form* in which to express himself, he dissipates his energies and does not devote enough attention to a careful study of the literary text which has been assigned. If the student can learn from the discussion of a technical problem, therefore, and can compare this discussion with a sample theme, he will set his mind working in the right channels and produce superior themes.

Though for illustrative purposes the sample themes are slightly long, they are within the approximate lengths of most undergraduate themes. The earlier themes tend to be short, while the later, more technical ones are longer. Although the various lengths cannot always coincide with the word limits set by individual instructors, the organization and method of the samples should be, and have been demonstrated to be, helpful. These samples should be regarded both as goals toward which the freshman can work and as guides for more advanced students.

The chapters have been arranged in order of difficulty and probable frequency of assignment. Although a full year's course could be devoted to the progression of themes from beginning to end, you may wish to assign the same type of theme on different works of literature until the students show mastery over that particular type. In whatever way the assignments are used, however, they offer a thematic unity to an entire year's course in composition—namely, writing themes about literature. In addition, I believe that the student beyond the freshman year will continue to find the book useful, because the advanced assignments here are as difficult and technical as those given in later courses.

The book offers a practical solution to a very real problem of many composition courses. Composition is frequently regarded as a service, for it teaches writing techniques essential in all college work. This need has forced the content in composition to cover too wide a range of subject matter. There can be little unity when students write themes on topics derived from many unrelated fields. All this material is usually taught by instructors who have been prepared by years of literary study. Here is the rub: although you yourself may want to teach literature as a discipline and as a pleasure, you know that your students must have intense work on composition for all their other college work. One purpose of this book is to reconcile this conflict by unifying the course and making it challenging to you as well as to the student. Using the assignments here, you can satisfy the needs of your course by teaching composition while you satisfy your own discipline by teaching literature and literary techniques. Although these assignments attempt to integrate the teaching of literature and composition, many of them have a residual effect upon other courses. For example, the lesson learned from the comparison-contrast theme can be applied to the heredity-environment controversy in a psychology or sociology class. Or the themes on tone and point of view will benefit the student of political science who must read and analyze speeches.

The book offers an almost foolproof solution to another difficulty in teaching composition—plagiarism. During one semester, for example, you might assign a theme about the main idea in "The Garden Party," while during the next you might assign a theme about the main idea in *Macbeth*, and so on. In colleges and universities where a common syllabus is used throughout all freshman courses, the same procedure could be followed uniformly. This plan, whereby the form of each theme is preserved while the subject material is changed, could render extinct the traditional fraternity-house theme barrel. The possibilities for varied assignments are virtually endless.

Most important of all, however, is that the book is aimed at the appreciation of good literature. Literature is the property of all; its appeal is to all. But literature, as an art, employs techniques and offers problems that can be understood only through analysis, and analysis means work. To help the student in this work is the immediate aim, but the primary object of the book is to promote the pleasurable study and, finally, the love, of literature.

To the Student

$\mathcal{E}$ ACH time you write a theme, you should consider the following points. A theme should be a short, accurate, and forceful presentation of ideas or descriptions, well contrived as a totality or unity. A theme should not ramble in any way, but should be clearly united around a dominating thought or *central idea*. A theme is a brief "mind's full" on any particular subject; that is, it presents the subject and considers this subject in several of its various aspects. The theme cannot cover all aspects, however, as might a book or long essay.

There are two basic needs that you must always remember. The first is for a *central idea* or *point* and the second is for a *clearly ascertainable organization*.

THE CENTRAL IDEA OR POINT

Themes are so named because throughout the composition called a *theme* there runs a basic or central idea—a theme—which unifies the paper into a logical whole. On every subject you encounter there should be some dominating idea or mood that will suggest itself to you, or that you will derive from your own intensive concentration. For example, when you look at a room, you might feel that it is cheerful; when you listen to the latest news, you might decide that it is depressing. Were you to write a theme describing the room or another discussing the news, you would have to keep your *central idea* foremost in your reader's mind *throughout* your theme, or else you would not have a theme.

You should first bring out your *central idea* in the introduction. State your point clearly, for your reader must be left in no doubt about what you wish to assert. Your point might be that "the story is well unified," or that it is "the folly of attempting what is beyond man's power," or that it is "the necessity for dedication regardless of the consequences," and so on. Throughout your theme, you must constantly keep reminding your reader of the relevance of your material to the point you have made; you must always emphasize the connection between your dominating idea and whatever you are saying at the moment. Anything not relevant to your point does not belong in the theme.

The need for a central idea will also make you aware of the need for paragraph transitions, because you are proving or showing *one* central idea, not a *number* of ideas. Transitions form bridges to connect one part of the theme with another; having a central idea always in mind makes continuity between paragraphs both essential and natural.

ORGANIZING YOUR THEME AROUND THE CENTRAL IDEA

Once you have thought of a central idea, you should make notes of materials which will support it. You will need to treat these materials in order, and in your introduction you should write a sentence that describes this order. This sentence is called a *thesis sentence*. Thus the introduction has importance for your whole theme: first, because it announces the central idea, and second, because it announces the pattern of the theme, through which the central idea should be carefully woven. As the whole theme is organized around the thesis sentence, each paragraph should be organized around a *topic sentence*. Here is a brief outline, to illustrate the meaning of these terms:

THEME

My Idea of a Good Book

Paragraph 1. INTRODUCTION containing CENTRAL IDEA and THESIS
SENTENCE
CENTRAL IDEA: A good book is a joy forever.
THESIS SENTENCE: A book gives me joy if it has realistic characters, a
plot which I can believe in, and an idea that is im-
portant to me in my own life.
Paragraph 2. TOPIC SENTENCE: Realistic characters stimulate my curios-
ity and imagination.
Paragraph 3. TOPIC SENTENCE: A believable plot makes me regard the
book as serious and important, not trivial.
Paragraph 4. TOPIC SENTENCE: An important and vital idea gives me
joy and also gives me something to ponder long after I put
the book down.
Paragraph 5. CONCLUSION

This illustration shows, in its simplest and most rudimentary form, the function of the thesis sentence and topic sentences in organizing a theme, and demonstrates the relationship between the two. Of course, as you become more experienced, you will vary these elements in your theme, making them more subtle and less obvious. They are here explicitly stated for purposes of illustration. Because the thesis sentence and topic sentence are basic concepts in composition, and are sometimes regarded as interchangeable, they are constantly distinguished throughout this book.

THE MAIN PROBLEM IN WRITING

Once you have understood and applied the principles of thematic development and thesis-sentence organization, you will still be faced with the problem of how to write well. There is little difficulty in recognizing superior examples of student writing when you see them, but there is usually much difficulty in understanding precisely what constitutes the superiority. For this reason the most difficult and perplexing questions you will ask as you write are these: (1) "How can I improve my writing?" or (2) "If I got a *C* on my last paper, why wasn't the grade a *B* or an *A*? How can I improve my grades?" These questions are really both the same, with a different emphasis. Your concern, therefore, is with improvement.

As an undergraduate, you should not be offended if you are told that you probably do not have a great deal of knowledge and understanding of literature. Your mind is growing, and it still has many facts to assimilate and digest. As you accumulate these facts and develop your understanding, you will find that your ease of expression will also develop. But at the moment your thoughts about literature might be expressed thus: "When I first read a work, I have a hard time following it. Yet when my instructor explains it my understanding is greatly increased. I would like to develop the ability to understand the work without my instructor's help. How can I succeed in this aim? How can I become an independent reader?"

In answer, you started trying to overcome the problem the day you enrolled in college. This action testifies to your desire to improve. Bear in mind also that education is a process, and that what baffled you as a freshman may seem child's play when you are a junior or senior. You will grow.

But in the meantime you want to know how to assist that growth. There is no magic answer, no short-cut to knowledge. You must work. In your literature classes, here are some habits that you should develop and always pursue.

1. Study each reading assignment carefully. Look up all words that you do not know.
2. For further study, underline what seem to you to be key passages. Write some of these passages out on cards, and carry the cards with you. Then, when you are riding or walking to class, or at other times, try to memorize key phrases and sentences and lines of poetry.
3. Make notes on interesting characterizations, events, and ideas. If you like a character, say so, and try to describe what you like about him. If you dislike an idea, say so, and try to describe what you dislike about it.

4. Try to see patterns developing. Make an outline of the story or main idea.
   What are the conflicts in the story? How are these resolved? Is one force, or
   side, triumphant? Why? Or is the conflict unresolved?
5. Do you see anything in the story that you do not understand? Do not forget
   the difficulty; write a note about it and ask your instructor in class.

The second major obstacle to writing well is inexperience. As a result,
when you start you may be tempted simply to write a *summary* of the
story or argument. A summary of a work is inadequate for your themes,[1]
mainly because a summary does not indicate real *understanding*.

Your education is aimed first at the *acquisition* of knowledge and
secondly at the *digestion* and *use* of knowledge. A summary indicates
only that you have read the material. Therefore if you wish to show your
understanding, you must do something more—you must show that you
can put what you have read into a meaningful pattern.

The theme assignments in this book are designed to help you do just
that. As you work out each assignment, you will be dealing with particular methods of assimilating and using knowledge. In only two assignments
are you asked to provide a summary: one is a *summary theme,* which
emphasizes that you organize your theme around a point, and the other
(the *general critique* or *book report*) employs a summary only as a brief
section. In all the other assignments you are asked to concentrate upon
discussing a particular point raised in the study of literature. In every
case it is important that you read and follow the work, but it is more
important that you show your understanding of the work.

There are a number of ways in which you may set up patterns of
development that can assist you in avoiding mere summary. One student
may make a deliberate point of discussing the conclusion of a story *first;*
in this way he can break the rigid order of following the story from first
to last, and can thus impose his *own organization* upon the theme. Another student may write to a mythical reader who has just finished reading the assigned work, but who has not yet had time to think about it
and understand it fully. Then, when this student-writer writes, he does
not need to tell his imaginary reader *what* happens, but can concentrate
instead on *why* things happen. This method has proved extremely successful. Let us look briefly at two examples of student writing to see how
this writer-reader frame of mind can operate to improve writing. These
examples are from themes analyzing Thomas Hardy's story "The Three
Strangers."

1	2
After a short lapse of time, the sec-ond stranger enters. He tells the	Hardy deepens his plot with the entrance of the second stranger—a

---

[1] Unless, of course, your assignment is to write a summary *theme.*

guests that he is en route to Caster-bridge, and he relates his occupation by singing a song. The second stran-ger is the hangman who is supposed to hang a man in Casterbridge for stealing sheep. As he reveals his oc-cupation, an air of dismay is cast upon the guests.

brash, selfish, demonlike figure who reveals in a grim song that he is a hangman. Since he is going to Cas-terbridge to hang a man for stealing a sheep, his manner fills the shep-herds, poor themselves, with dismay. Hardy must have a purpose in this response. I believe that it is to de-velop both sympathy for the shep-herds and anger toward inhumanity in the law.

The first column is adequate but no more, for it illustrates only super-ficial knowledge. The second column illustrates *understanding* and is therefore superior. Phrases like "Hardy deepens his plot" and "Hardy must have a purpose" illustrate that the writer of the second column is assuming that his reader knows the plot and wants the story interpreted.[2] Notice too that the second column is more compressed than the first, even though it is longer (78 words to 62). Its greater length is caused by greater *play of mind* (to borrow a phrase from Matthew Arnold). Com-pare again the information contained in these two parts of the paragraph:

. . . the second stranger enters. He tells the guests that he is en route to Casterbridge, and he relates his occu-pation by singing a song. The second stranger is the hangman . . .

. . . the second stranger—a brash, selfish, demonlike figure who reveals in a grim song that he is a hangman. Since he is going to Casterbridge . . .

The subject matter of the two passages is essentially the same, but the second column says, in twenty-six words, more than the first column does in thirty.

The answer to that difficult question about how to make *C* writing into *A* writing is probably to be found in the comparison of the two columns. Besides using English correctly, the superior writer always allows his mind to play upon the materials. The superior writer always tries to give the results of his thoughts to the reader. He dares to trust his responses and is not afraid to go out on a limb. When he refers to events in a story, he embodies observations and interpretations in his remarks. Observe that there is a play of mind operating in this sentence, though the sen-tence also refers to events:

Since he is going to Casterbridge to hang a man for stealing a sheep, his manner fills the shepherds, poor themselves, with dismay.

---

2 Unless you are writing a summary theme (see Chapter 1), you should always assume that your reader has read the work you are discussing (see also, in this respect, Chapter 2).

Notice the words "since" and "poor themselves." These have been introduced by the writer to indicate relationships—causes and effects. There is simple knowledge here, but, more importantly, there is also *use* of this knowledge. If the quality of good writing can be located, it resides in the inclusion of words of this sort and in the understanding shown by that inclusion. If you wonder how to improve your writing and your grades, the answer is: work constantly toward writing that will demonstrate your *understanding*. Grammar, organization, central idea—all these are important, but all are subordinate to understanding.

Whenever you write a theme about literature, then, you must strenuously try to show your understanding. Your greatest problem is that of unity. Once you have gone off on a tangent, you are following the material rather than leading it. If you can stick to your point, however, you will be mastering the material and thereby showing understanding.

Let us look at another example. The following paragraph is taken from a theme on the "Idea of Personal Responsibility in *The Odyssey*." This is the third paragraph; the writer has stated his thematic purposes in the first paragraph, and in the second has shown that various characters in *The Odyssey* believe men are responsible for their actions and must bear the consequences. In the third paragraph he writes:

> More forcefully significant than these statements of the idea is the way it is demonstrated in the actions of the characters in the epic. Odysseus, the hero, is the prime example. Entrapped by Polyphemus (the son of Poseidon the Earth-Shaker by the nymph Thoosa) and threatened with death, Odysseus in desperation puts out the eye of his captor, who then begs his father Poseidon for vengeance. Answering his son's anguished curse, Poseidon frustrates Odysseus at every turn in the voyage back to Ithaca, and forces him to wander for ten years before reaching home.

This paragraph shows how easily a person may be diverted from his objective in writing. The first sentence adequately states that the idea is to be demonstrated in the actions of the epic. That the remainder of the paragraph concentrates upon Odysseus is no flaw, because the writer concentrates upon other characters in following paragraphs. The flaw is that the material about Odysseus does not go beyond mere summary; it does not come to grips with the announced topic of personal responsibility; it does not indicate understanding. The material may be relevant to the topic, but the writer does not point out its relevance. The writer began well, but he did not show how the material illustrates his point, and thus the total paragraph is bad. Remember always that in expository writing you should not rely upon making your meaning clear simply by implication; you must make all relationships explicitly clear.

Let us see how this problem can be solved. If the ideal paragraph could be schematized with line drawings, we might say that the paragraph's topic should be a straight line, moving toward and reaching a specific goal (explicit meaning), with an exemplifying line moving away from the straight line briefly in order to bring in material, but returning to the line after each new fact in order to demonstrate the relevance of this fact. Thus, the ideal scheme would look like this:

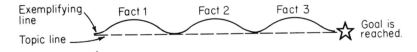

Notice that the exemplifying line, or the example or the documenting line, always returns to the topic line. A scheme for the paragraph on *The Odyssey,* however, would look like this:

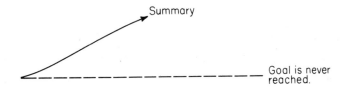

How might this paragraph be improved? The best way is to reintroduce the topic again and again throughout the paragraph, in order to keep reminding the reader of the relevance of the exemplifying material. Each time you mention the topic, you are bringing yourself back to the line, or back to the point, and this practice should prevail no matter what the topic. If you are analyzing *tone,* for example, you should keep pointing out the relevance of your material to the tone of the work, and the same goes for *structure* or whatever aspect of literature you are studying. According to this principle, we might revise the paragraph on *The Odyssey* as follows, keeping as much of the original wording as we can. (Parts of sentences stressing the relationship of the examples to the topic of the paragraph are italicized.)

More forcefully significant than these statements of the idea is the way it is demonstrated in the actions of the characters in the epic. Odysseus, the hero, is the prime example. When he is entrapped and threatened with death by Polyphemus (the son of Poseidon the Earth-Shaker by the nymph Thoosa), Odysseus in desperation puts out the eye of his captor. Though his action is justifiable on grounds of self-preservation *he must, according to the main idea, suffer the consequences.* Polyphemus begs his father Poseidon for vengeance. Poseidon hears, *and accordingly this god becomes the means of enforcing Odysseus' punishment,* since Odysseus, in injuring the god's son, has insulted the god. The Ithacan king's ten years of frustration and exile are therefore not caused by whimsy; *they are punishment for his own action. Here the idea of personal responsibility is shown with a vengeance;* despite the extenuating circumstances, *the epic makes clear that characters must answer for their acts.*

The paragraph has been lengthened and improved. You might object that if all your paragraphs were lengthened in this way your theme would grow too long. The answer to this objection is that it is better to develop a few topics fully than many scantily. Such revision might therefore require you to throw away some of your topics, or else to incorporate them as subpoints in the topics you keep. This process can only improve your theme. But the result of greater length here is that the exemplifying detail points toward the topic, and the paragraph reaches its goal.

Whenever you write you should keep this lesson in mind. Keep returning to the point you wish to make; regard the material of the work you have studied as material to prove your point, not as material to be described; keep demonstrating that all exemplifying detail is relevant to your main point. If you observe these precepts, you should be well on the way toward handling any of the following theme assignments successfully.

Writing Themes
About Literature

1

The Summary Theme

HOUGH not often assigned, the summary theme is one of the more important themes you can write. First, it indicates to your instructor that you are able intelligently to follow a literary work and that your basic understanding of the work is clear. Second, the summary theme represents a building block for other kinds of themes. Before you write about the structure of a poem or novel, for example, you must be sure that you understand the main idea and the story; otherwise, everything you say is likely to be inaccurate or misleading. The ability to summarize, in short, anticipates all the other writing about literature that you will do.

The first requirement for writing a summary theme is to read the assigned work carefully: be sure to take notes on the important events or ideas; be sure to look up all words that you do not know; be sure that you are able to understand the special context of the work. Without a knowledge of the context, you can get into difficulty. For example, a student once interpreted Wordsworth's poem "The Solitary Reaper" as Wordsworth's celebration of the advent of the industrial age, since this student thought all the descriptions referred to the McCormick reaper! If he had provided himself with a wider context by reading even a few of Wordsworth's other poems, he would have avoided this absurdity.

WHAT DO YOU SUMMARIZE?

Once you have collected your notes on the work, you face the fundamental problem of what, exactly, to summarize. This problem may seem simple at first glance, but the experience of many students has shown otherwise. Most defects in summary themes result from an apparently imperfect idea of what is needed. You can solve the problem—and produce a good summary theme—if you keep the following in mind; in the literary work which you will be asked to summarize, there are two major elements that you should consider. The English novelist E. M. Forster has conveniently classified these elements.[1] The first is the *story,* or the main

---

[1] *Aspects of the Novel* (New York: Harcourt, Brace & World, Inc., 1927), p. 130.

1

events, details, or happenings in the work, as they appear in chronological order. The second is the *plot,* or the reasons or logic underlying the story and causing that story to take the *form* it does. There is little question, of course, about what happens in the story, since all the events are in front of your eyes, and can easily be verified. But there is more room for interpretation and subjectivity about the plot, because the reasons for which characters do things are not always clear, even to the characters themselves. To write a good summary *theme,* you must not only summarize the story, but also must convey to your reader an explanation of why the story is as it is—in short, you must treat the plot as a part of your summary. It is also essential to convey an idea of the organization of the story. All these must be included in your summary theme.

Indeed, the principal danger in writing a summary theme is that you will neglect the plot and organization. It is entirely possible, for example, to summarize the main events without ever giving a hint of why those events take place. The objection to a simple summary of events is that it gives the impression of low understanding. However, if you assume that your reader has not read the work you are summarizing, you will realize that he wants to know not only the events (story), also also the reasons why the events happen (plot), and that he will also want to have some rudimentary idea of the organization of the work.

You must therefore study your notes on the story or play carefully. Observe whether the events you noted fit into any sort of pattern. What seem to be the main points of the story? How do these events fit the main points? In *Oedipus Rex,* for example, you might determine that the events occur as part of a plan to illustrate Oedipus' pride; that is, you might say that all the events in the play are either caused by his pride or cause him to realize his pride; his realization may be regarded as the climax of the play. In whatever work you have read, you must decide what the main points are and what events are important in the making of these points. Above all, remember that events in works of fiction do not simply happen; they are always put in by the author as part of a plan or idea. *Discover that plan or idea.*

PLANNING YOUR THEME

Once you have made your decision about the main idea of the story, you arrive at the recurrent problem of organization. Remember that you are writing a summary *theme,* and that a theme by definition must contain a dominating plan or idea. Remember also that your theme will be considerably shorter than the work you are summarizing, and that your theme is *not* that work, but is *your own.* All statements that you make must necessarily be your own, with the exception of short quotations from the text (which are desirable). In short, though what you say is *about* the original, it is your own work and must necessarily be *unlike* the original.

All these considerations will make you realize that when you write any theme you must be in charge and remain in charge. Therefore, you must decide what will be *your* central idea, which will be your idea of the most significant point in the work you have read (e.g., "In this novel the main theme is the growth from childhood to adulthood," or "In this play the main character realizes the folly of trying to set himself above Fate," and so on). Without doubt it is difficult to make sure that your interpretation of the main point will coincide with that of your instructor, but remember that he will prefer any interpretation to none at all. You should attempt an interpretation, and use it as the central idea in your theme. So long as you are consistent in using your central idea throughout your theme, your instructor will honor your interpretation. Where you can go wrong is not in your interpretation, but in failing to maintain that interpretation as a central idea everywhere in your theme; in that event, it is your theme, not your interpretation, that is bad.

You should state your central idea in a thesis sentence, which will (a) state the plan of the work, and also (b) organize your own theme and enable you to bring out your central idea. A thesis sentence might be, "This growth is described by Mark Twain in an extensive trip on a raft down the Mississippi River, where numerous adventures cause the narrator, Huck, to grow to maturity despite the restrictive background from which he has come." Once you have decided upon a central idea and thesis sentence, fill in the details of your theme and do the job of writing it.

WRITING THE THEME

In writing you need to follow through with your plan as outlined in your thesis sentence, and to include enough detail to bring out your central idea. If you were summarizing *Huckleberry Finn,* for example, you would build upon the thesis sentence by mentioning (a) the early events before the trip, and (b) the principal events on and off the river, in such a way that you would emphasize Huck's increasing maturity. Naturally you cannot summarize everything in the story; nor would everything be desirable, for your mythical reader could go to the novel itself if he wanted to know everything. Your use of topic sentences will help you here, for if you say that "The first part of the work describes the common sense of Huck when he is faced with Tom Sawyer's mental extravagances," then you do not need to describe every detail, but only the most significant ones. Similarly, after you have discussed the "first part," let us assume that there is a second, or third, or fourth part. Before you start summarizing each part, it is absolutely essential that you inform your reader of the new section. Then you need to include only as much detail as exemplifies your topic sentences. The object of your theme is to summarize, accurately, the work of literature assigned; the problem is to stay in control of the material, not merely to say "This happens" and "That happens," but instead to say "This happens as part of this pattern," and "That happens as part of that pattern." Control the material; do not let it control you.

How much detail should you include? You must give your reader as thorough, but as brief, a knowledge of the work as is possible within the limits of the assignment. If a man is murdered in your story, it is worth saying that "X shoots Y, who dies," or if a man steals a horse, it is interesting and perhaps important to say "Z steals Sheriff Q's horse." Unless details of this sort are essential, however, you should not lengthen your theme by including them. For example, in the ancient *Epic of Gilgamesh* (which is the topic of the sample theme), the hero Gilgamesh is reverent toward the gods and goddesses Anu, Shamash, Ishtar, and Ninsun, but in a summary theme there is no particular advantage in including these names; it is therefore wise simply to say that the hero is pious or reverent. In this way the point is made without the inclusion of interesting but unnecessary details. The intelligence you show in selecting details—distinguishing the essential from the nonessential—will be extremely important in the quality of your finished summary theme.

THE ORGANIZATION OF YOUR THEME

There will usually be two parts in a summary theme.

Part I: Introduction

The introduction identifies the work, the most significant character or characters, and the general situation; it also states your central idea and your thesis sentence.

Part II: The Summary

The summary itself grows out of your thesis sentence. The development of your theme should follow the form of the work that you are summarizing. Remember that what characterizes your theme *as a theme* is your central idea—your general interpretation of the work—and your guiding topic sentences that give unity to each of your paragraphs. Remind yourself constantly as you write that (a) you should closely follow the work you summarize, (b) you should write accurately, precisely, and vividly, and (c) you should use an occasional word, phrase, or passage from the work in order to give your reader at least a taste of the original.

A NOTE ON THE FOLLOWING SAMPLE THEME

In the sample theme, the *Epic of Gilgamesh* is discussed in the expectation that this work is unfamiliar to you. You will presumably begin reading this theme in a state of ignorance similar to that of the reader for whom you design your own summary theme. You should observe in the sample that the thesis sentence and the topic sentences give you understanding of the epic's major parts, because all the events could not, and should not, be summarized. It is hoped that this sample will help you see the necessity of a thesis sentence and topic sentences in your own theme.

The Epic of Gilgamesh is one of the oldest stories in our literary tradition. It apparently was first inscribed in the third millennium B.C., and was known by most of the peoples in the ancient Near East. The fullest surviving version is in a number of cuneiform clay tablets from the library of the Assyrian king Ashurbanipal (668–626 B.C.).

Sample Theme

The Story of *The Epic of Gilgamesh* [2]

Gilgamesh, the hero of this ancient epic, is part god and part man. He is the pious king of the city-state of Uruk, and is a great builder and dreamer. Of great but at first unguided power, and with burning vision, Gilgamesh is humanized by his friend Enkidu, and after his friend's death he searches for answers to life's mysteries, which always elude him.

The first three divisions in the modern edition of the epic make up a first half, which is about the beauties of friendship and the greatness of human curiosity and valor. At first, Gilgamesh is a despot. His oppressed subjects pray for relief, which the gods give to them in Enkidu—a natural, innocent demigod who lives and runs among wild animals. Hearing of the danger, Gilgamesh by a clever ruse deprives Enkidu of his natural, animal power. But Enkidu is still a threat and attacks Gilgamesh. Though Gilgamesh wins the fight, the two demigods learn quickly to respect each other's valor. Under the influence of Enkidu's moral strength and advice, Gilgamesh becomes just and wise. In other words, the epic seems to say that through humanity and friendship comes justice.

---

2 N. K. Sandars, trans., *The Epic of Gilgamesh* (Baltimore: Penguin Books, Inc., 1960). All page numbers in this theme refer to this edition.

But there is also greatness, and Gilgamesh wants it. His ambition is to break through into unknown territory, and with Enkidu he embarks upon an adventure into "the land of the cedars" (i.e., the forests of Lebanon). Fame is his desire; Shamash, the Sun-God, is his guide. After conquering the protector of the forests—the giant Humbaba—Gilgamesh strips the forests of trees, presumably to build Uruk into a great city. In short, ambition and piety combine to produce greatness.

At the end of all greatness, however, there is death, the theme on which the first part closes and with which the second will be occupied. Because Gilgamesh and Enkidu kill a bull sacred to the goddess Ishtar, the gods decree that Enkidu must die. Enkidu is quickly stricken with illness; he languishes and dies. In mourning and despair, Gilgamesh concludes that "the end of life is sorrow" (p. 90).

The second part, dealing almost exclusively with the themes of human fragility, frustration, and grief, continues the mood of sorrow but evolves to triumph. Lamenting his friend's death, Gilgamesh determines to seek the immortal Utu-Napishtim, who lives in Dilmun, the garden of the sun, and to ask him for the secret of everlasting life. Though Gilgamesh is told that he will never find this life, he is resolute: "Let my eyes see the sun," he says, "until they are dazzled with looking. Although I am no better than a dead man, still let me see the light of the sun" (p. 97). After discouragement and difficulty, Gilgamesh reaches Utu-Napishtim (the ancient Assyrian equivalent of the Biblical Noah), whose narrative is lengthy. Generations earlier, Utu-Napishtim had been chosen by the God-of-the-Sweet-Waters, Ea, to preserve all species. *Seven* seems to be Utu-Napishtim's magic number: seven days of building the boat; six days of storm and a seventh of calm; seven days aground on Mount Nisir before learning that the flood has receded. As reward, the Earth-and-Air-God En Lil gave Utu-Napishtim eternal life. It is to obtain this secret that Gilgamesh has traveled to Dilmun.

As the epic constantly shows, however, all human dreams come to nothing. Gilgamesh gains the secret of eternal life—an underwater plant —but it is stolen from him by a serpent. There is nothing left but death for our king. Returning to Uruk, he quietly succumbs to the inevitable and almost automatic death which, try as he might to avoid it, was always his destiny.

With the hero dead, the conclusion of the epic is a sombre and beautiful meditation upon death, which is always man's portion:

> The king has laid himself down and will not rise again,
> The Lord of Kullab will not rise again;
> He overcame evil, he will not come again;
> Though he was strong of arm he will not rise again;
> He had wisdom and a comely face, he will not come again;
> He is gone into the mountain, he will not come again;
> On the bed of fate he lies, he will not rise again,
> From the couch of many colours he will not come again.
>
> —pp. 116–117

The poem thus concludes on the ideas that life is brief and filled with sorrow, that the desire for power does not satisfy, and that the quest for eternal life cannot succeed. Therefore, man's noblest achievement is justice to others during life.

2

The Report, or The General
Critique of a Literary Work

$\mathcal{J}$HIS assignment will generally be given with the direction simply to "Write a report or paper about such-and-such a story, novel, poem, or play," or "In this course you will be expected to submit an X number of book reports." Assignments of this sort will be made not only in literature courses, but in many others. For such an assignment, you are generally on your own and, since what to say is entirely up to you, you may understandably feel ill at ease. "What should I say?" "How should I organize the material?" "Should I write a summary?" "What does my instructor want?" "And he's the one who talks about being specific." Reactions like these naturally arise if you have received no other directions.

As you begin to think and to write, you should consider the subject of your theme in the following light: though your instructor has made a general assignment, he probably wants to see evidence that (a) you have read and followed the work, (b) you have understood it and can say something intelligent about it, and (c) you have reacted to it in some way and have formed an opinion about it. Assuming that your report is well written and punctuated correctly, the quality of what you write will depend upon the success with which you fulfill these three requirements.

In order to demonstrate understanding (the second requirement), you must *analyze* the work in question. The primary analysis you do here anticipates all other analysis you will do later. Before we turn to the instructions for writing the general critique, then, a discussion of literary analysis is in order.

WHAT IS LITERARY ANALYSIS?

Analysis tries to find truth. The process of analysis is to divide a problem into various parts, for, while a whole object is difficult to comprehend at one glance, the parts may be examined more easily, and their natures,

8

functions, and interrelationships may be more fully understood when they are examined one by one. For example, if you have the problem in chemical qualitative analysis of discovering the elements in a chemical solution, you can make only one test upon the solution at a time, because if you tried to make all your tests at once you would not be able to control or distinguish your results.

The analysis of literature is based on the same truth. While the work you have read is an entirety, you must make separate inquiries in order to discover its full meaning and to appreciate it fully. You could not talk about everything in *Paradise Lost* at once, for example, without being guilty of the greatest superficiality. It is better, in your discussion, to narrow the scope of your topic by talking about the diction, epic conventions, theology, dramatic action, and so on. An attempt to discuss everything at once would inevitably distort some things and omit others; results of this sort of investigation are usually wrong or at best misleading. Truth, on the other hand, can emerge only where all possibilities are considered. Therefore, your problem in making an analysis is to keep the limits of your investigation to a size small enough to permit you to consider all the possibilities. In other words, you can write a good theme about a relatively restricted part or aspect of the work you have read, but would find it impossible to discuss everything unless your analysis extended to the length of a book.

A serious objection sometimes arises about literary analysis. Although scientific analysis is necessary, it is said that too much literary analysis "spoils" appreciation of the work, or that, in making an analysis, you "murder" literature as you "dissect" it. This objection is valid only if you substitute literary analysis for literary appreciation. It is therefore important that you keep literary analysis in perspective: analyzing a work is a *means* toward appreciation and evaluation, not an end in itself. It is an honest attempt by you, the reader, to discover the truth about a work, and to base your appreciation upon your own thought and discovery, not upon a vaguely aesthetic reaction. If you analyze the work to know it better, and therefore to like it better, you have really dismissed the entire objection.

As you think about what to put into your theme, remember that literary analysis is a way of getting at the heart of the work. To this end, there are four broad areas which literary analysis explores: (1) meaning, (2) structure, (3) style, and (4) background and influences. There is usually overlapping among these; for example, in writing about *point of view* you would emphasize its impact upon both meaning and style. In discussing background and influences, you might emphasize how things seemingly extraneous to the work enable a fuller comprehension of meaning, structure, and style. It is always wise, in fact, to emphasize that your particular topic has a relation to the entire work, for in this way you are really demonstrating the relationship of literary analysis to literary appreciation.

For your book report, you are only concerned with literary analysis in a general sense, so that you may make your analysis simply by answering key questions (the study of background and influences will probably not even be requested or desired in this type of theme). When you were reading the work, did you notice that the author emphasized any particular ideas? This question of course concerns *meaning,* and to deal with it properly you must (a) state the ideas, (b) show their relationship to the work as a whole (i.e., show how the ideas influenced organization and style), and (c) evaluate the ideas *as* ideas. Similarly, did you notice the form or organization of the work (a *structural* question)? To deal with this question you ought to describe the organization, then show *why* the organization is as it is, and finally show either that the organization is good or that it could have been better. You might also deal with the issue of whether the author used particular stylistic devices to convey his ideas; he may, perhaps, have used dialogue, indirect discourse, understatement, and irony. In poetry it is sometimes helpful to count stanzas, lines, and words; analyzing or parsing sentences may also yield insights that you did not have when you first read the work. Did you notice any particular words that seemed pre-eminent (style)? What was the nature of these words (style)? Did they form part of a noticeably definite pattern (style and structure)?

The analytical section is the place for you to bring out these and similar observations.

THE ORGANIZATION OF YOUR THEME

You should include the following parts in your paper:

A Short Summary

The remarks about the summary theme also apply here. The summary should take up no more than one-fifth of your theme. (This proportion will be smaller in longer reports, in which most of your attention should be devoted to analysis.) Remember that an intelligent summary should be interpretive in a limited way; this one should almost exclusively summarize *plot,* as distinguished from *story.* If the work you are analyzing is divided into parts, chapters, stanzas, or some other ascertainable divisions, your summary should take these matters into account. The summary should also rely upon short quotations from the text in order to root itself as deeply as possible in the original work.

An Analysis

In this section you analyze the principal meanings and qualities of the literary work. This section should occupy the largest part of your theme: about five-eighths to three-fourths. Your instructor will probably place greatest weight upon the skills you show in this section. You should therefore be at pains to demonstrate that you have examined the assigned text closely and that your understanding is beyond what is required simply for following the idea or story.

When you write, you might try to answer many questions, or perhaps only one, depending upon the nature of the questions. If you deal with a question about ideas, for example, your analysis might very well be taken up entirely with that question. You may prefer to write on style, structure, and meaning separately. One thing to bear in mind, however, is the general nature of the assignment: if you discuss a main idea, it is wise to show how that idea affects and is affected by the style and structure. You are concerned here with the general technique of literary analysis; the more specific techniques will come later. Show that you are a good, alert reader and your book report will have achieved its aims.

Although you must remember that your instructor is looking for evidence of your alertness, you should not regard *him* as the reader whom you are addressing. Imagine instead that your reader is another student like yourself, a student who has read the same work but has not understood it. Now, how can you justify writing unless you are going to tell this mythical reader something he does not know? You must tell him something new; you should be constantly trying to acquaint him with insights and understanding that he may not have had. *Insight* is the key word. Look at the text, and look at it again; think, and think again; then tell your reader of the results of your vision and thought. The really original part of writing about literature—and expository writing in general— lies in your power to acquaint your reader with your insights, and as you succeed in conveying them you will discover that writing of this type is challenging, creative, and exciting.

You can make this section unnecessarily difficult if you allow yourself to wander. You must always remember that a theme should have *thematic development* (see "To the Student," pp. xvii). Your analysis should therefore be tied to the summary, perhaps by introductory remarks like "As this brief summary shows, X-author's dominating idea was that . . ." (then would follow your analysis of that idea); or "This work's outstanding quality, which my summary cannot show, is the uncanny way Y-author's style creates a powerful effect upon the reader . . ." (then would follow an analysis of how that effect is created), and so on. Throughout the section you should make sure that your sentences have relevance to some central point. All your insights, word counts, and general brilliance will lose value if they do not cohere to a definite point. In short, your analysis should show continuity and development.

The Final Section: Your Attitudes

Your theme should conclude with an explanation of your attitudes toward the work (about one-fourth to one-eighth of your theme). Although not the largest in terms of space, this section is nevertheless important. In view of what has been said previously about literary analysis, it seems natural to consider your attitudes toward the work as a concluding section of your critique. Your remarks here should take on greater weight because of your work on the analysis. It is usually gratifying to describe your own opinions when they are based on calm, rational thought, not prejudice. (Prejudice is usually the result of unconsidered emotion. It might lead to your rejecting a poem "because I don't like poetry." A considered opinion, on the other hand, is the result of thought; it might result in your criticism of a work because it does not succeed in doing what it tries to do, and so on.)

Your likes and dislikes have a definite place in this section, though, if you combine them with your judgment to answer questions that are really important. How did the literary work affect you? Did you feel satisfied, complete, happy, after reading it? Did you think that the work was good? Bad? Did you feel that the author should have done something more? This section is the place for your individual thoughts and reactions. Do not be afraid to speak your mind, but do not do so unless you have a sound basis in ideas from the text. Good literature is always interesting and moving, and it should be enjoyed by all. If the particular work did not affect you, therefore, it is your duty to say so, but try to assess the blame for failure properly: if you did not like the work, is the fault in you or in the work? In dealing with these questions, you will perhaps learn something about yourself, but you will also be dealing with questions of *evaluation* and *appreciation*. These words are fundamental to the study of literature. You will quickly see that this third section, instead of being the easiest, is the hardest of all, because evaluation and appreciation are not to be taken whimsically. When you write about literature more frequently, you will also notice that your evaluative powers will increase as you develop into a more disciplined reader.

CAUTIONS

These, then, are parts of the *general critique* or the *book report*. This type of theme is not vague, but extremely specific. What you say is up to you, as long as you say it about the work assigned, and as long as you remember that your instructor is interested in seeing (a) the evidence of your general analytical ability, and (b) the nature and degree of your individual reactions. Remember that good writing is always your aim. Make your theme coherent; be sure that your paragraphs start with transitional phrases. Your theme will have three parts, but do not make them seem like three lumps. Work out a good thesis sentence that will assist your reader to understand the organization and plan of your paper, and write a brief but interesting introduction. In short, keep in control at all times.

Keep in mind that this suggested organization should be adapted to the specific directions of your instructor. If there are no other directions, the three parts of the general critique should give you an acceptable organization and should enable you to write a well-rounded theme.

PROPORTIONS

The suggested lengths for the various parts will hold good for most assignments in freshman and sophomore classes. In more advanced classes, however, the proportions of the first and third sections will frequently be lessened and the second section will frequently be expanded. Your instructors in these classes, should they make an assignment of this type, will want evidence of your analytical abilities. They will usually take for granted your ability to summarize a work and to appreciate it.

Sample Theme

A General Critique on Wordsworth's Sonnet "Composed Upon Westminster Bridge"

At first glance this sonnet seems unlike the usual Wordsworth poem. "A poem about a bridge? In a city?" might be asked by a reader believing that Wordsworth was strictly a poet of Nature. Fuller reading, however, forces us to modify our understanding of *Nature* as it applies to Wordsworth's poem, for this short piece is about a broader conception of Nature than just flowers and forests. To show this point, after I briefly describe the contents of the sonnet, I will analyze some of the means by which Wordsworth brings out these impressions. No reading of the poem can avoid touching upon one's beliefs and reactions, and so a discussion of this effect is also in order.

In the first eight lines (the octave) of the sonnet, Wordsworth describes London as he saw it from the top of a coach riding across Westminster Bridge early on the morning of September 3, 1802. His opening sentence, that "Earth has not anything to show more fair," is augmented by another statement that the "sight" is "touching in its majesty"; Wordsworth implies that anyone who would not be thus affected must be a clod. In the glorious morning light, the poet states, all the commonplace buildings of London take on a "bright and glittering" quality.

In the concluding six lines (the sestet), Wordsworth describes the impact that the scene has made upon him: (a) the city is more beautiful than any natural landscape, (b) the scene has made him feel the deepest calm of his existence, (c) the river, in obeying its current, seems like a thing alive, with a will, and (d) the houses seem to be similarly alive, but are now sleeping, just as the collective heart of all sleeping Londoners is at rest.

This description shows that Wordsworth is actually more concerned with his own reactions to the scene described than with the scene itself. In the poem, only four lines out of the fourteen are descriptive of anything visible (lines 6, 7, 10, 12), and even these are highly subjective. The remaining ten lines are all occupied with Wordsworth's reactions to the scene. It is interesting to observe that in this poem, the product of a poet whose aim was to keep his eye always upon the subject, there are many abstract words in key positions: *fair, dull, touching, majesty, beauty, beautifully, splendor, calm, sweet, seem, mighty*. The total effect of these words is to convey a relatively inexact picture but a vivid impression, an impression which conveys the idea that there is more to the city asleep than just silent houses and splendid sunlight. This "more" fits into my general point.

For Wordsworth is actually personifying the city, in this way broadening his definition of *Nature* to include man and man-made things for their human worth and power. The city is like a human being (the central part of Nature) and is valued for this similarity. It is alive. "Like a garment" it wears "the beauty of the morning." Wordsworth draws our attention away from the more concrete implications of this comparison by the previously mentioned abstractions. Like all his poems, this one is finally about the "grandeur in the beatings of the heart" (*Prelude,* I, 414).

The city has a heart, and even a soul, and as it takes on these qualities it illuminates our understanding of Wordsworth's scheme of Nature. How does this process work? Like this, I believe: all the sleeping Londoners share one common thing—a life principle. They share this principle with the birds, flowers, trees, and beasts which make up Nature in the more primitive sense. Thus, if Nature—the universe—is mystically pervaded by the "motion" and "spirit" that roll "through all things" (*Tintern Abbey,* lines 100, 102), so also is the city pervaded with this spirit because of its being a part of Nature. It seems that something like this process of reasoning has quietly overwhelmed the poet in the concluding lines:

> Dear God! the very houses seem asleep;
> And all that mighty heart is lying still! [1]

---

[1] *The Poetical Works of Wordsworth,* 2nd ed., Thomas Hutchinson and Ernest de Selincourt, eds. (London: Oxford University Press, 1953), p. 214. All quotations refer to this edition.

The sleep is significant because when the city is asleep it is much closer to its fountainhead of virtue—direct communication by way of the soul with the "Wisdom and Spirit of the Universe" (*Prelude,* I, 401) —than when it is awake. When men are awake, they resist Nature, but when they sleep, the barriers to Nature are removed; imagination takes over; unconsciousness takes over, and Nature can then bring mankind back to herself. Because of this process the sleeping city is almost a holy thing to Wordsworth, since sleep is actually a means by which Wordsworth's belief in the restorative, recreative power of Nature takes place. Nature virtually works right in front of the poet's eyes. Is it any wonder that he firmly states:

> Ne'er saw I, never felt, a calm so deep!

The poem thus arouses deep questions about life that most of the time are obscured by the round of daily activities. To us sleep is sleep; to Wordsworth sleep is a restorative both to the sleeper and to the viewer in the early morning, since it links God and the Universe with man. My thinking on this subject has been disturbed by scepticism supported by the failure of any signs to appear to me. What impresses me about Wordsworth, however, is that he can make so much of material that to me is simply ordinary. He sees signs where I do not. Yes, I would perhaps say "It's a pretty morning," if I were to see a similar sight. But I could never verbalize my impression the way Wordsworth does (Wordsworth would probably say that I would still benefit greatly from my impression). Does my inability mean that Wordsworth is wrong about his philosophy? In sceptical moments my answer is "yes." But a rereading of the poem makes me realize that there may be more to sunlight steeping a city than is dreamed of in my philosophy. Wordsworth begins with ordinary things, but because of his power to see he is great. His poem widens out into an unexpected vista which previously I had not seen. "Composed upon Westminster Bridge" is great, not only because it has this width, but also because this new vista has emerged from the inescapable world of fact. That the fact—London, September 3, 1802—exists or existed is as certain as any fact can be; that the unseen world discussed by Wordsworth is always present cannot therefore be overlooked. His poem is always there as testimony to his main idea: man is part of divine existence which comprises Nature in the highest sense.

3

The Theme on a Close Reading
of a Passage or Work:
The Analytical-Reading Theme

*Y*OUR main task as a reader is to understand and appreciate the page in front of you. Beyond the words, phrases, clauses, and sentences are implications, shades of meaning, beauty. For a full understanding and appreciation you should, theoretically, spend as much time reading a work as the author spent writing it; that is, you should spend this much time, using all your alertness and skill, if you really want to grasp everything. Time, unfortunately, is prohibitive, and therefore you must settle for something less. With good reading skills, however, you can perceive and appreciate a great deal of the expressed and implied meaning.

To assist you in developing good reading techniques, your instructor will probably spend much classroom time in explicating, and discussing with you, various poems, novels, plays, and stories. As you experience this classroom guidance, you should develop the ability to read well without guidance. The theme asking you to perform a close reading of a passage is therefore an important means by which your instructor can verify your progress as a reader.

The close-reading theme is an assignment very much like the middle section of the general critique (see chapter 2), except that it is usually confined to a brief passage. Unlike the theme on a specific problem (see chapter 4), it indicates your *general* perceptions as a reader, and is not confined to a single issue.

The assumptions behind the close-reading theme are these: if you can read a page, you can read the entire book of which the page is a part; if you can read a speech, you can read the entire play; if you can read one poem by a poet, you can read all the poems by the same poet. Underlying these assumptions are others: in a good literary work, each part is absolutely essential; nothing could be eliminated without damage to the work. In the same way, all the writings of each author form a homogeneous unit, with each work contributing something to that unity. A close reading of an individual passage, therefore, or of an entire work, should indicate essential truths about the work or about the author being studied. Your reading of a passage or of a poem should indicate your ability to handle entire works.

A close reading of a passage requires a certain awareness of *style* and *prosody* (see chapters 13 and 14), but your focus in this theme will only touch upon these elements indirectly. Instead, you are to focus attention upon everything in the passage or work assigned. If the work is particularly rich in meaning, you will need to select from the superabundance; if the work seems thin, you can cover everything. Works by good writers, however, generally offer God's plenty for your study.

VARIOUS ASSIGNMENTS

A close-reading theme will frequently be assigned in courses in drama or the interpretation of poetry, although it can be assigned in any course, including courses in novels and short stories. Your instructor will give you the assignment as "Write a paper on this passage," or "Write an analysis of this poem." When you have received this assignment, you have the job of writing a theme based on close reading.

Though you are concerned here with writing a theme, you might be given the assignment as part of a classroom impromptu or examination (see Appendix A, on tests). Either you might be required to analyze a poem or passage, or you might be given a number of passages as identification-and-comment questions. If you have a passage to identify, concentrate upon its subject matter and position in the work and in the philosophy of the writer.

PREPARING TO WRITE

Your first job is to read the entire work in order to make sure that you understand the relation of the passage to the whole. If you do not read the entire work first, you are likely to make inexcusable blunders in your reading of the specific passage. Read carefully. Then study the passage you are to write about. First, be sure to use the dictionary for all words that are even slightly obscure. Sometimes you may not be getting the sense of a passage at first or even second reading. Remember that even the simplest looking words may offer difficulties. Therefore, you must look up *all* the words in the passage that is giving you trouble, and frequently you will discover that your trouble resulted from attaching the incorrect meaning to a word. Use the dictionary whenever you have the slightest question. In Shakespeare's sonnet No. 73, for example, this famous line appears:

> Bare ruin'd choirs, where late the sweet birds sang.

If you regard *choirs* as an organized group of singers (as you are likely to do at first), you simply will not understand the line. The dictionary will tell you that *choirs* may be an architectural term referring to the part of a church in which the singers usually are placed. Let us take another line, this time from John Donne's first Holy Sonnet:

> And thou like Adamant draw mine iron heart.

Unless you look up *Adamant* and realize that Donne uses it to mean a magnet, you are likely not to know the sense of *draw,* and you will thus miss the meaning of the entire line.

You also ought to use your imagination to find whether the words in the poem or passage convey any consistent patterns, as a pattern of references to flowers, to water, to high finance, or to political life. In your preparation for writing, do not hesitate to pick out such references in each line. Try to classify them into categories, for you can frequently achieve an extremely good reading by making drawings and schemes.

Once you have understood the words, pay some attention to the sentence structures, particularly in poetry. If you read the line "Thy merit hath my duty strongly knit," be sure that you figure out the proper subject and object of the verb ("Thy merit hath strongly knit my duty"). Or, look at these lines:

> Let such teach others who themselves excell,
> And censure freely who have written well.
> —Pope, *Essay on Criticism,* lines 15–16

On first reading, these lines are difficult. A person might even conclude that Pope is asking the critic to censure (For an assignment, look up *censure* in the O.E.D.) those writers who have written well, until the lines are unraveled thus:

> Let such who themselves excell teach others,
> And let such who have written well censure freely.

There is quite a difference here between the correct reading and the misreading. What you must keep in mind is that your failure to understand a sentence structure that no longer exists in everyday English can prevent your full understanding of a passage. Therefore you must be absolutely sure, in your preparation, that you have untied all the syntactic knots.

With this preparation done, you may go on to plan and write your theme.

THE FORM OF YOUR THEME

Introduction

Your introduction should describe the particular circumstances of the passage or work. Who is talking? To whom is he talking? Under what circumstances is he talking? Why? What is the general subject matter of the passage or work? These questions are relevant to whole poems as well as to fragments from a drama or story.

When you have answered these questions, you should make plain your central idea. Never begin to write until you have developed a general reaction to the passage or work assigned; your description of this reaction will be your central idea. The sample theme argues that in the passage analyzed Hamlet is speaking about himself—giving a self-revelation, as it were. The remainder of the theme develops this idea. In a theme showing a close reading it is sometimes difficult to arrive at a central idea, but if your theme is to be good, you must produce some guiding point that makes sense out of your reading.

Body

Your plan in the body of the theme is to combine the results of your close reading with the central idea you have asserted. You might be guided by the following:

SPECIAL CIRCUMSTANCES Observe the special circumstances of the passage or work to see how they influence the language, and therefore how they illustrate your point (e.g., suppose that the speaker is in a plane crashing to the ground; or suppose that he is on his way to meet his sweetheart; either of these circumstances must be mentioned and kept in mind throughout your discussion). The sample theme analyzes Hamlet's disturbed state of mind when he is addressing the ghost, who has just left the stage. The presence of the ghost is a special circumstance which accounts for Hamlet's shock and confusion.

DICTION Discuss the meaning of the words as related to the speaker's background and state of mind. In Browning's "Soliloquy of the Spanish Cloister," for example, the speaker is a jealous, worldly monk. His language is the kind a monk might use, but his interjections and schemes all show that he is a spiteful, petty person, certainly not a saintly, holy one. The language in Keat's "Ode to a Nightingale" indicates that the speaker is in despair, disappointment, and uncertainty, but it also shows his joy in life's fullness and in the beauty provided by the imagination.

The sample theme demonstrates that Hamlet's diction is that of a student; therefore it is natural for him to use the references to *tables* in the academic sense.

When you discuss diction it is also proper to make observations on both the direct statements in the work and the implications and suggestions. Also, if there are any special problems with words, describe these problems and show how their solution (by aid of the dictionary) has assisted you in your reading.

OTHER ELEMENTS   Discuss all other things which are relevant to your point. Here you might include any or all of the following:

1. Any noteworthy ideas. Your emphasis, however, should not be on the ideas *as ideas,* but on the way they are related to the central idea of your theme. For example, the sample theme briefly discusses the Renaissance theory of faculty psychology, but relates this theory to the central idea of Hamlet's self-revelation.

2. The sentence patterns and rhythms of your passage. Because this analysis is fairly technical, it anticipates the prosodic analysis of poetry and the stylistic analysis of prose. In the present theme, however, you need to show only those qualities of style and versification that are relevant to your point. The sample theme demonstrates that at the end of the passage there are falling, trochaic rhythms which are sympathetic to the spirit and mood of Hamlet's speech. By emphasizing relationships of this sort, you can make your discussion of technique contribute to the thematic unity of your paper.

3. The relationship of your selection to the rest of the work. Here you would be pointing out the work's organic nature, because you would be emphasizing that your passage is *essential* to the whole. The sample theme asserts that the passage in question is the climax of the first act of *Hamlet,* and that it predicts much of Hamlet's future action.

Conclusion

In a theme of this type there is little need for a formal conclusion, particularly if you have been allowed a limited number of words. You have indicated your ability to read a page, and should feel gratified that you have succeeded. Though there is no need for an elaborate conclusion, you ought to provide a clear restatement of your central idea. The last sentence should make your theme sound as though it has ended.

A NOTE ON MECHANICS

For easy, quick reference, you should include a copy of the passage you are analyzing. Regardless of the numbering in context, you should number your passage beginning with *1*. These smaller numbers are easier to manage in your theme than the larger ones, particularly if you mention several at a time. Whenever you quote from your passage, indicate in parentheses the line number of your quotation. Should your passage be prose, number the lines as they fall in your duplication.

Sample Theme

Hamlet's Self-Revelation:
A Reading of *Hamlet* (I, v, 95–109 [1])

Remember thee!	1
Ay, thou poor ghost, while memory holds a seat	2
In this distracted globe. Remember thee!	3
Yea, from the table of my memory	4
I'll wipe away all trivial fond records,	5
All saws of books, all forms, all pressures past,	6
That youth and observation copied there,	7
And thy commandment all alone shall live	8
Within the book and volume of my brain,	9
Unmix'd with baser matter. Yes, yes, by heaven!	10
O most pernicious woman!	11
O villain, villain, smiling, damned villain!	12
My tables, my tables—Meet it is I set it down	13
That one may smile, and smile, and be a villain!	14
At least I'm sure it may be so in Denmark.	15

In this passage from Act I of *Hamlet,* Hamlet is alone on stage immediately after the ghost has left, and so the character addressed is the ghost, at least at first. Actually, however, the speech is a soliloquy, since Hamlet almost immediately seems to be talking to himself, or to the open air. Though Hamlet speaks about the ghost, his mother ("O most pernicious woman"), and his uncle (the "villain"), the real subject of the speech is himself. Clearly, his words describe his state of mind; his selection of words indicates his background as a student, his awareness of what is happening to him, and his own highly agitated mental condition at the moment.

For Hamlet has clearly been disturbed by the ghost's message that Claudius is a murderer. While previously the young prince has been melancholy and ill at ease, feeling the need to do something but without any reason for action, he has now realized that definite action will be necessary in the future. His desire for revenge here reaches the fury that he will later feel in the "rogue and peasant slave" soliloquy. His

1 *The Complete Plays and Poems of William Shakespeare,* William Allan Neilson and Charles Jarvis Hill, eds. (Cambridge, Mass: Houghton Mifflin Company, 1942), p. 1056.

passionate dedication to vengeance is sworn "by heaven!" His disturbance, which he himself recognizes in line 3, is demonstrated first by his
decision to wipe away "all trivial fond records" from the "table" of his
memory (5, 4), and then by his writing down (or so we presume) in his
"tables" (i.e., his commonplace book, his notebook) that "one may
smile, and smile, and be a villain" (14). Can this distinction between
his declaration and his action do anything but indicate his mental confusion?

Regardless of this confusion, Hamlet's selection of words related to
tables indicates that his existence as a character has been completely
visualized and perfected by the dramatist, Shakespeare, who has created
a diction that is in perfect accord with Hamlet's background as a
student. Hamlet's speech is therefore the most telling indication that
his subject is really himself. *Table, records, saws of books, copied, book
and volume of my brain, baser matter, tables, set it down*—all these
smack of the classroom, where Hamlet has so recently been occupied.
And in lines 2 through 10 there is a complicated but brief description
of Renaissance psychology, obviously a subject which Hamlet has just
been learning, presumably, at Wittenberg. Briefly, he states that his
mind, or his memory, is like a writing tablet, from which he can erase
previous experience and literature (the "pressures past" of line 6), and
which he can then fill with the message which the ghost of his father
has just transmitted to him. In short, his mind will never be quite the
same, since the new message will occupy it entirely.

Once Hamlet has decided to erase all previous impressions, it is as
though he has killed his past, and, once he has made his resolution,
his future project will be to murder Claudius. It seems deliberate,
then, that the last lines of this passage are characterized by many
trochaic rhythms, which would have been described in Shakespeare's
day as having a *dying fall*. There are falling rhythms on *yés, bý
héavèn*, and *O víllain, víllain, smíling, dámnèd víllain!* The last two
lines end with trochees (*víllain, Dénmàrk*). This rhythm is unlike most
of what went before, but will be like most of what follows, particularly
the interjections in the "To be or not to be" soliloquy and the conclusion in that soliloquy (on the word *action*).

Since this passage reveals Hamlet's character so clearly, it is startlingly
relevant to the rest of the play. From this point onward Hamlet will
constantly be spurred by this promise to the ghost, that the ghost's
"commandment all alone shall live / Within the book and volume of
. . . [his] brain," and Hamlet will feel guilty and will be overwhelmed
with self-doubt and the urge for self-destruction because he does not
act upon this promise. His attitude toward Claudius, which previously
was scornful, will now be vengeful. His attitude toward Ophelia will
be blighted by his obsession with vengeance, and as a result Ophelia,
a tender plant, will die. Truly, this passage can be regarded as the
climax of the first act, and the prediction of the remainder of the play.

4

The Theme on a Specific Problem
in a Literary Work

HIS theme assignment is a catchall type frequently assigned in literature courses. It differs from the book report (or general critique) because it is devoted to providing a solution to a specific problem, not to a discussion of the literary work by a summary, analysis, and report of your reactions. Perhaps the best way to think of the specific-problem theme is to compare it to the analytical section of the general critique except that you are here devoted to solution of a specific problem, while your discussion in the general critique is generally expository. Your method, of course, will depend upon the problem you attempt to solve. Some problems require simple exposition; others require an argument attempting to prove or disprove a certain controversial point.

Problems occur in all human activities, of which literature is only one. The passive reader is aware of few problems in anything, but the active reader—which you are trying to become—is inquisitive. He constantly asks questions like "What does this mean?", "Why is this here and not elsewhere?", "What would this work be like without that?", and "What would this character do in other circumstances?" As he raises these questions, he learns about art and broadens his general ability to read and think, while the passive, unquestioning reader sits back and never realizes what he has missed. The solution of problems in literature, just like the solution of scientific problems, is a basic and necessary part of your education.

HOW ASSIGNED

The problems you deal with in this type of assignment may be assigned by your instructor (for both papers and tests), or they may arise in classroom discussion. Suppose that a particular question puzzles the members of your class. You might well find yourself with that problem as the subject of your next theme.

23

You might also be asked to make up your own problem for a theme assignment. In this event you must conceive of a problem and formulate it. Write down all questions that occur to you as you read. You might easily make one of these the problem you deal with in your theme. Here also you can use your classroom experience, for in the classroom your instructor will have been raising problems regularly. His hope is that the experience of classroom discussion will help you eventually to develop feelings for the relevant sorts of questions that you yourself should raise. Now, suppose that in class you have discussed a work in which the principal character is under a sentence of death. What questions arose? How were these questions answered? By contrast, suppose that the work which you have been assigned concerns people with an undetermined future (e.g., "they lived happily ever after"). Can you raise problems about this work similar to those that were raised in class? Or, suppose that in class you have discussed a comic work, and have answered questions about what makes it comic. If your assigned work is comic, you might bring some of the classroom discussion to bear upon a problem of your own about the causes of laughter.

In brief, if you have been put on your own resources for this assignment, try to use what you have learned in the classroom. In this way, you will be reaching one of the goals of your education—the ability to make independent inquiries.

YOUR PROBLEM IN WRITING THIS THEME

Your main job in this theme is to provide a convincing solution to the specific problem with which you are faced. You must perceive the most significant implications of the problem and decide upon a suitable order in which to deal with them. Then you must judge the relevance of materials from your text. Choose only those that have an immediate bearing upon the problem. Of course, both your sharpness as a reader and your close study of the text will bear fruit here, because much material seemingly irrelevant to a careless reader can be interpreted as vital by a keen, knowledgeable reader. As in all your assignments, your first objective is therefore to think carefully.

THE NATURE OF LITERARY PROBLEMS

Problems may be of any kind, and in this respect all writing about literature may be fitted into the *problem* category. For convenience, the problems may be classified as *artistic* (concerning style, arrangement, and general content), *conceptual* (concerning ideas), and *historical* (concerning influences, background, and genre).

You should realize that a problem will often cause a fusion of these three classifications, because they are all interlocked in the literary work itself, and because the problem may certainly be relevant to any and all classifications. You should also realize that your method of handling the theme will depend upon the way in which the problem is put. For example, the question "What is the influence of the pastoral machinery upon Milton's 'Lycidas'?" would require an expository treatment of how the pastoral elements figure in the poem. The aim of a theme on this problem would be mainly expository. But a related problem might be "Does the pastoral convention spoil 'Lycidas' by making it seem too artificial?" You can see that writing a theme on this second topic would require argument rather than simple exposition. Naturally a certain amount of exposition would be necessary in the treatment of this problem, but the exposition would be used only as it related to the argument. (A way of handling this problem is shown in the sample theme.)

Artistic Problems

Almost anything in a literary work can be dealt with in artistic terms, but you are here concerned with problems as they relate to matters of style, structure, and—by extension—motivation and character. Suppose, for example, you were asked the question, "What meaning does the name 'Joe Christmas' have in the novel *Light in August* (by William Faulkner)?" This question is directed toward the novel, and implies that you would answer it as it relates to the artistry of the novel, even though in doing this job you would need to answer the question of Faulkner's idea in the novel. If you interpret Christmas as a "reverse image of Jesus Christ" (as some critics have done), then it is necessary for him to be killed at the end, if your parallel is to be exact. Your consideration would therefore involve you in a discussion of *structure*.

As another case, suppose you ask why Browning, in "The Pied Piper of Hamelin," created "such a rhythmic verse and such happily jingling rhymes." To solve this problem, you would need to decide how true the assumption about the verse is, and then relate the quality of the verse to Browning's subject and intended audience (the subtitle "A Child's Story" suggests that the poet had a certain audience in mind). Your method, as you see, would not be simply to analyze and scan the verse, but to bring to bear the results of your analysis and scansion upon your conclusion.

Similarly, suppose you ask why the Polyphemus episode appears where it does in Odysseus's narrative in *The Odyssey*. Solving this problem really involves a discussion of *structure* in relation to your interpretation of the epic. Your solution might be something like this: "Since Polyphemus's curse is the cause of Odysseus's ten-year journey, it must come at the beginning of his wanderings, after his leaving Troy. Also, if *The Odyssey* is to some degree a story showing how Odysseus's ideas of personal responsibility grow, Odysseus must have time to recognize his guilt where Polyphemus is concerned, and must also reconcile himself to what is essentially a tragic view of life."

You can see that dealing with a problem like this also involves a consideration of motivation and, necessarily, of character. If your problem, for example, is to answer the question of "How does X change in the work?" or "Why does Y behave toward Z as he does?" and so on, you are dealing with causes, effects, and relationships among characters. All these problems are artistic.

Conceptual Problems

Problems of this sort are about ideas. Your intention in dealing with a problem about ideas, however, is not expository, but argumentative. After reading Aldous Huxley's novel *Point Counter Point,* for example, you might ask how valid his ideas are about the role of politics in modern life. This problem requires not only that you describe Huxley's ideas on the subject (perhaps as expressed through the character Mark Rampion), but also that you criticize these ideas, showing their validity and perhaps stating the degree of their applicability to modern society. And, if you conclude that they are not applicable, what other answers might be more applicable? You can see that solving a problem about ideas sometimes requires subjective responses from you; on many occasions you might dispute with your author, at other times you might agree with him. How, for example, would you solve the problems implied in "Wordsworth's ideas on 'The Old Cumberland Beggar' and modern welfare"? Or try "Did the ideas of Dos Passos on politics really change from *U.S.A.* to *Mid-Century?*"

Historical Problems

Most problems of this sort require a certain amount of research. Suppose that you are dealing with a problem of influences (you should know that many instructors object strongly to the assumptions underlying the word *influence,* and would probably not give you such an assignment). You are given the problem of Virgil's influence upon Chaucer. You probably could not solve this problem yourself, and so would have to consult a secondary source or sources in your library. If this problem were put in a different way, however—let us say "The similarity of ideas in certain works by Virgil and certain works by Chaucer"—you could probably solve the problem yourself by recourse to a comparison-contrast method, though you would certainly not claim that one poet influenced the other. Even in this inquiry, however, you would probably help yourself by using a secondary source. (A *secondary source* is a book *about* the works or authors you are reading; a *primary source* is usually the work itself.)

Problems of *background* and *milieu* also require varying degrees of research. Background information about the position of the Jewish people in medieval history would assist you in solving a problem like "How did Chaucer's audience interpret *The Prioress's Tale?*" *Milieu* refers to the intellectual and artistic currents prevailing at the time of a particular writer. If you were asked to solve the problem: "What was the milieu of Shaw's *Mrs. Warren's Profession?*" you would need research in secondary sources to help you with your answer.

A similar need to do research would occur in problems of *genre* or *type.* As with *influences,* the study of genre has fallen into some critical disrepute. But if you determine the genre of a work, you will know what to expect from it, and can thereby make a reasoned evaluation. It would be folly for you to read a Greek tragedy and compare it unfavorably with *Hamlet* because "*Hamlet* has more action than the Greek tragedy, and besides, the Greek choruses are dull." You must understand that Greek tragedies had different conventions from those in Shakespeare's plays; a consideration of genre would therefore permit you to understand the differences and lead to a better appreciation of both kinds of plays. As another example, you may fail to appreciate certain works of poets who wrote during the neoclassic period of English literary history. A realization that these writers wrote according to rules of genre would make you able to recognize the requirements which they set for themselves (i.e., epic satire, Horatian satire, mock-epic satire, pastoral poetry, discursive poetry, heroic drama). Once you recognized the limits of their achievements, you would be better able to recognize their merits. In this way, the study of genre brings a wider range of appreciation than you could gain without it. Remember one thing, however: when genre leads to unwarranted conclusions (for example, pleading that because Housman was a great poet within the limits he set for himself he is to be regarded as Milton's equal), it has defeated its own purpose—reasonable appreciation.

In dealing with a problem of genre, then, you will need to learn the special conditions under which the work was composed, and the type that the work was supposed to be. Some problems of genre would be: "*Hamlet* as a revenge play," "*Gulliver's Travels* as a travel book," "Dryden's *Annus Mirabilis* as a 'historical' poem," "*An American Tragedy* as a realistic novel," "*The Nun's Priest's Tale* as a beast epic," "*The Rape of the Lock* as a mock-heroic poem," and "Virginia Woolf's *Mrs. Dalloway* as a stream-of-consciousness novel." Your problem would be to set up an idea of what to expect from the work which you have considered, and then to show how it successfully lived up to these expectations.

Problems of genre can also require a treatment employing argument. For instance, "To what extent is *Gulliver's Travels* more than just a

parody of contemporary travel books?" or "Did the revenge motif in
Hamlet limit Shakespeare in treating Hamlet's responses to Claudius?"
Questions like these can be multiplied indefinitely. In dealing with one
of them you would (a) examine the truth of the assumption about genre,
and (b) deal with the relationship of the genre to the problem at hand.
Such a method is seen in the sample theme, where the pastoral genre to
which "Lycidas" belongs is related to the quality of the poem as a poem.

YOUR APPROACH IN WRITING

As you may conclude from the types of problems discussed, it is impossible to predict all the various problems that will occur not only in
your classes but also in your mind as you read literature. For your theme,
however, remember the following: Your job is to convince your reader
that your solution to the problem is valid. Your theme will therefore
most often require an argument designed to support your central idea
(which is in fact a short statement of your solution to the problem). The
various parts of your theme will be subpoints supported by evidence.

As you read your literary work, take notes on relevant details. Study
your notes carefully after you have finished reading. From your notes you
should arrive at a major conclusion, which you will make the central
idea of your theme. The material in your notes may then be arranged in
an order suitable to the logical steps of your argument. When you begin
to write, you may suddenly realize the importance of other material that
you did not include in your original notes. Work in this new material,
but take care to illustrate its relevance to your central idea.

Depending upon the degree of argument required by your topic, you
will find a need to examine closely the key words in the statement of your
problem. It is always wise to study these words carefully. If your instructor
has phrased the problem for you, his phrase may contain words having
implications with which you do not agree. That is, some of his words
may "beg the question." You will also find it necessary to determine the
limits within which you wish a certain word to operate. Or, if you object
to the way in which a problem is phrased, you may wish to rephrase it.
What would you do, for example, with problems phrased like these: "How
much misanthropy does Swift show in *Gulliver's Travels?*" or "Show why
Faulkner is the great American novelist." You can quickly see that these
are "loaded" questions. To answer the first you would need to determine
the meaning of *misanthropy* and, if you admitted the word at all, you
would need to limit its use to Swift's meaning. For the second question
you would need to spend time on the meaning and admissibility of the
phrase *is the great* before you could write a good theme. The sample
theme considers the assumptions underlying the word *artificial* when ap-

plied to "Lycidas." This theme accepts a favorable connotation of the word, but asserts that the pejorative connotation does not apply to Milton's poem. To a great degree, the theme develops from this analysis of the word *artificial* and its implications. You might profit from employing a similar method whenever you are confronted with a literary problem of this nature.

As with all themes except the summary, you may assume that your reader has knowledge of the literary work you have read. Your job is to arrange your materials convincingly around your main point. You should not use anything from the work that is not relevant to your central idea, regardless of where it appears in the work. You do not need to discuss things in their order of appearance in the work. You are in control, and must make your decisions about order so that your solution to the problem may be brought out most effectively.

THE ORGANIZATION OF YOUR THEME

Introduction

If your problem requires an examination of any of its key words, the introduction is the proper place for this examination. Once that is done, your introduction should describe the problem in terms of either its importance in the work you have read or its general importance in life and literature. Thus, say you have the problem: "Is Moll Flanders's bad life justified by her economic circumstances?" You might wish to look first at the phrase "bad life," and may conclude that it is properly descriptive. Then you might wish to deal with the issue of justification in either or both of two ways: (a) whether, and to what degree, the immediate circumstances justify the sins of which Moll is guilty; (b) whether environment is generally a justification for human conduct. Ultimately, you might find yourself raising other perplexing moral and artistic questions which develop from these, for once you have raised the original problem, more problems usually follow, and they should be used to strengthen your argument. Though the original problem is particular, then, it raises general implications that should also be dealt with if a solution is really to be found.

Your introduction should also describe your solution to the problem in a brief statement, which will be your central idea. Your thesis sentence should conclude the introduction.

Body

The body should contain the main points of your argument. Another way to look at the body is to think of it as stating the main reasons for which you have arrived at your solution. Generally, you will state a point (topic sentence) and then show how a certain amount of representative material from the work supports that point, and so on throughout the body. Always keep emphasizing, however, how the material supports your point. Just to present the material is to write a summary, and this theme is not a summary.

Conclusion

Your conclusion should affirm your belief in the validity of your solution in view of the supporting evidence. You must recognize that in non-scientific subjects like literature there are rarely absolute proofs, so that your conclusions will not actually be proved. But your conclusions, along with the evidence, should be *convincing,* and you should always give the impression that you have not been grinding an axe. The conclusion of your theme should therefore build conviction in your reader. If there are any doubts that you think might still be in his mind, you should satisfy these doubts in your conclusion. It is therefore a good rhetorical method to answer any objections or contrary claims that might be raised against your solution. Whether you phrase the objections fully yourself or only make them implicit, you ought to answer them. In this way you convince your reader that your solution has been reasoned out wisely, and that you have left no stones unturned in seeking out evidence and in thinking of solutions.

Sample Theme

Does the Pastoral Convention Spoil "Lycidas" by Making It Seem Too Artificial?

This question can be dismissed easily by the asking of other questions: should *artificiality* be admitted as a spoiling element in art? Should art have no art at all? Obviously the answer to both these questions is "No," and a thundering "No!" at that. I find it impossible to believe that art can exist without a great element of artificiality; art needs the control of a shaping spirit, and without this control it is not art. If I imagine what the simple report of a man's day would be like, I find it dull. The report needs *form* and *style,* and both of these are *artificial* in the best sense of the word. The question of artificiality, therefore, is a false one.

The original question may be admitted to have validity, however, if by *artificiality* is meant a quality of unnaturalness. If the pastoral convention provides nothing more than a pretty, formal facade, behind which there is no substance, then the original question may be answered "Yes." But I believe that "Lycidas" is a poem of great substance, and that its pastoralism adds to this substance. The pastoralism gives perspective. It elevates the tone, and gives what might have become simply a personal effusion a universal meaning without sentimentality. Certainly, the pastoral convention does not spoil "Lycidas," but helps to make it great.

Milton gains perspective, and thereby universality, through the pastoral machinery. One of the underlying ideas of his poem, for example, is that he himself might be stricken dead in the bloom of youth before he has had a chance to make his mature contribution to the ages, just as Edward King (Lycidas) had been killed before he fulfilled himself. Milton's first expression of this idea occurs in lines 64 through 84. These lines do not concern the speaker directly, but are taken up instead with questions of why a young man should "tend the homely slighted shepherd's trade, / And strictly meditate the thankless muse." [1] If a young man is to die before fulfilling his aims, in other words, he might as well enjoy himself with Amaryllis and Neaera; if he is destined to make no mark in the world, he at least can have pleasure. The answer to these doubts is that the reward of the faithful, self-effacing shepherd is "fame in heaven" (84), and that even the attempt to be a shepherd is therefore good. Though it seems clear that Milton by the idea of *shepherd* had service to the Church in mind, it is also clear that, once the pastoralism is admitted to have symbolic meaning, the idea is also applicable to any young man with a sense of professional dedication.

Similar perspective is gained by the outburst of St. Peter against the many phony, undedicated shepherds who are seizing the rewards of service without rendering the service (lines 108-132). Here, Milton's complaint is no longer personal, but is directed against the entire class of bad clergymen who by neglecting their congregations permit a spiritual dry rot to overwhelm the country by default (127). The statement of this idea in the language of the pastoral, by its very indirectness, permits the inference that any profession at any time, whether religious, political, educational, medical, or what not, can be included in the condemnation of St. Peter, if it permits its membership to become corrupt.

For universalism of expression is finally the aim of "Lycidas," and the pastoralism permits this universality. When Milton describes the singing and dancing that he heard and saw around Cambridge he mentions no local names; his diction makes sure that his description is all-inclusive:

> Rough satyrs danced, and fauns with cloven heel,
> From the glad sound would not be absent long,
> And old Damaetas loved to hear our song.
>
> —lines 34–36

---

[1] Lines 65 and 66, in *The Complete Poetical Works of John Milton*, Harris Francis Fletcher, ed. (Cambridge, Mass.: Houghton Mifflin Company, 1941), p. 117. All line numbers refer to this edition.

The "grim wolf" in line 128, though usually interpreted as the threat of the Roman Catholic Church upon the English Church, can therefore be any threat that results from spiritual deterioration caused by corrupted leadership. In the same way, Milton causes a fusion of the Christian and the pagan Classical traditions; Christ, for example, has been called the *Good Shepherd,* and the Twenty-third Psalm states that "The Lord is my Shepherd." With these obvious parallels, Milton causes a gradual change from the pagan Orpheus in line 58 to "the dear might of him that walked the waves" in line 173. There are other connections between the pagan and the Christian, but the point is that by causing this fusion, through the pastoralism, Milton has attempted to make the poem valid for all ages and places. Presumably a person brought up in any religious faith, even a tree-worshipper, could see the general significance in Milton's poem.

One thing that seems clear from my examination of "Lycidas" is that any claim that the pastoralism spoils the poem is based on misreading. If it were claimed, for example, that "Milton and King never had anything to do with tending sheep," there is the obvious parallel that they both were young men of deep dedication who had in common their mutual concern for their church and their country. Or, if the claim were offered that the diction is unnaturally affected, this answer might be made: since Milton's speaker ("the uncouth swain") is conceived as a shepherd, any words that are not pastoral would be unnatural for him, and it would be affected for him to speak any other way. Moreover, the language keeps the tone high, in keeping with the themes of the pastoral elegy—death and the purpose of life. It might also be claimed that in "Lycidas" Milton did not show great feeling toward his dead friend. But Milton in fact shows much feeling, and the pastoralism keeps it from being personal and effusive.

In truth, the degree of Milton's greatness in this poem results exactly from the way in which he sees general problems resulting from his own, and the way he keeps from sentimentalism toward Edward King and from pity toward himself. The pastoralism permits him not only this control, but also the widest possible expression of this generality. Does the pastoral element spoil Milton's poem? It seems rather to make the poem into one of the greatest works in English literature.

5

The Theme About a Literary
Work as It Embodies Ideas

*T*HE WORD *idea* is closely related to the actions of seeing and knowing. It is therefore variously defined as a mental image, picture, or perception, and also as a concept, thought, opinion, or belief. This second meaning is the more widely held, and the one that will be used in this chapter. You may have expressed the idea that men are punished for their sins, or that they are not punished. This idea fits the definition of belief. Or you may have attempted to think of the idea of *freedom,* which is a concept about a desirable political and personal condition. These ideas are simple in the sense that they do not call forth reasoning. But the word *idea* may also refer to plans and schemes which are products of the thinking or reasoning process. Thus the idea of *democracy* is a complex one that involves a certain analysis and belief in human nature; it is a plan, based upon this analysis and belief, about proper political organization and operation to utilize the best in human nature and to control the worst. In studying literature you will encounter both simple and complex ideas.

You have spent much of your reading time in discovering and profiting from ideas, just as much classroom time on literature is devoted to the discussion of ideas. But bear in mind that, while ideas are important, they are not all. Try to find a "message" in Keat's "To Autumn," and you will realize that looking for ideas and *only* for ideas has limitations (e.g., searching only for ideas might make a reader oblivious to literary pleasures derivable from such things as the artist's diction, manipulation of sound, comic techniques, and control over structure). Within these limitations, however, the study of ideas is valuable. If you have been asked to write about ideas, your purpose should be to analyze the literary work in order to name, discuss, and evaluate the ideas contained therein. Usually it is best for you to concentrate on one major idea rather than several.

PROBLEMS

In expository literature there are few special obstacles to understanding the principal idea or ideas, because a major purpose of exposition is to lay out ideas. Except for the special kind of exposition known as dialogue, therefore, exposition offers only the ordinary difficulty of understanding the ideas as they are presented—a difficulty that every college student encounters when he listens to a lecture or reads a textbook.

In imaginative literature, however, which tells stories and presents attitudes, the perception of ideas is more difficult, since the ideas are usually presented indirectly and are therefore subject to interpretation. Though ideas are subordinate to the story, and though the story could be enjoyed without reference to them, the ideas are important reasons for which the writer has written the story, and sometimes they will have dictated the precise *form* or *structure* of a particular work. Analysis of ideas therefore anticipates discussion of the technical terms *plot* and *structure* (see chapter 12). You should also understand that ideas themselves are enjoyable in literature. The classical or "Horatian" view is that literature should be both pleasing and instructive. While some writers have denied one or other of the two aims (e.g., Poe, who said that literature should only please, and Shaw, who said that the only justification for literature was instruction), it is best to assume that these two functions are virtually identical. You should therefore realize that the analysis of ideas is a means of deepening your appreciation of literary works.

The analysis of imaginative literature for ideas is, in essence, the process of translating the concrete story into the usual language of ideas—namely, expository prose. You can easily see that one immediate difficulty of your analysis will be whether you are translating the story properly—whether you are reading the signs aright. Most critical divergences arise at this point. Remember, however, that your interpretation or translation will usually be respected, so long as you base your statements accurately upon the story itself. If for some reason you happen to make errors, either because of faulty understanding or because of your own prejudgments, you will of course be subject to correction. Be sure that your reading is accurate, and that your interpretation is not far fetched. Then you will have nothing to worry about.

Another difficulty that usually occurs is interpreting the extent to which a writer *intended* that you derive a certain idea. For example, there has been a long controversy over Shakespeare's idea about Shylock in *The Merchant of Venice*: did Shakespeare present Shylock as a farcical outsider in a Christian society, or as a sympathetic outcast and a victim of religious prejudice? Similarly, in reference to Shakespeare's *Henry V,* many critics have thought that Henry is engaged in a righteous war which brings out the valor and strength of the English people, and that he is one of England's great kings. But other critics have thought that Henry cynically embarks upon a war of aggression and is responsible for many needless deaths. These differences of interpretation bring up the question of whether the writer's intention is even relevant, because the author seldom states his intention explicitly.[1] Many critics have asserted that great works have new meanings for each succeeding generation, in spite of the writer's intention. Therefore you are free to look at the work itself and consider it primarily as a living work that is communicating ideas directly to you.

HOW TO FIND IDEAS

In reading any text for ideas your aim is to find and describe the ideas there. You should therefore know the ways, direct and indirect, by which authors express ideas. The following descriptions are for convenient analysis only, because in a literary work the methods described may all occur simultaneously.

DIRECT STATEMENTS BY THE AUTHOR   When an author states ideas in his own person you should consider these at face value. It is reasonable, when you discuss these ideas, to attribute them to the author. Remember, however, that your attribution should not have the weight of absolute biographical fact. You are reading an author's work, not his mind, and an author may well exercise his right to express ideas of the moment or ideas with which he does not agree. When in writing a theme you say "George Eliot believes," or "It is Faulkner's idea that," you must always realize the limitations of your statements: you are really not talking absolutely about the *authors,* but instead are talking about their *works.* With this reservation your remarks about an author's ideas should usually be acceptable.

DIRECT STATEMENTS BY THE AUTHOR'S PERSONA   Frequently authors, instead of narrating in their own persons, will write from the point of view of a character in the work (for example, Frederick Henry in *A Farewell to Arms,* and Gulliver in *Gulliver's Travels*). Such a character is called a *persona,* with life and independence of his own, and with the freedom to state ideas peculiar to himself. While the author unquestionably might agree with the ideas of his *persona,* you can never know exactly when this agreement takes place. Though the statements of a *persona* may be direct, therefore, you must use your ingenuity and intuition in deciding how closely the *persona's* ideas correspond with the author's.

DRAMATIC STATEMENTS MADE BY THE CHARACTERS IN THE WORK   In any

---

[1] See W. K. Wimsatt, Jr., "The Intentional Fallacy," *The Verbal Icon* (New York: The Noonday Press, 1960), pp. 3-18.

dramatic work, and in most novels, stories, and poems, the characters will state ideas. What the characters say will often be in conflict, for an author may sometimes present thirteen ways of looking at a blackbird, and leave the choice up to you. He may provide you with guides for your choice, however. For instance, he may create an admirable character whose ideas presumably coincide with his own. The reverse would be true for a bad character, and so forth.

CHARACTERS WHO STAND FOR IDEAS   The characters themselves often represent ideas. In this case, interactions of the characters may represent the interweaving of ideas, and the conflicts between characters may represent conflicts between ideas. For example, in allegories like *The Faerie Queene* and *Pilgrim's Progress,* the characters stand for ideas in conflict. Aldous Huxley, in his novels, has evolved a form called *the novel of ideas,* where the various characters in the story are made to represent ideas that in Huxley's opinion give his novels intellectual life.

THE WORK ITSELF AS IT IMPLIES IDEAS   Perhaps the most important method by which authors embody ideas in a literary work is to manage carefully the total impression of the work. All the events and characters may add up to an idea that is made particularly powerful by the emotional impact of the story itself. Thus, while an idea may never be stated in the work, it will be apparent after you have finished reading it. In the novel *A Passage to India,* E. M. Forster shows that political institutions and racial and national barriers prevent men from realizing that they are brothers. Though he does not use these words, this idea is clearly embodied in the novel, and your reading would be incomplete if you did not see this implication. Similarly, Shakespeare's *Hamlet* might be interpreted as an illustration of the idea that evil breeds evil upon evil, sweeping both the innocent and guilty before it. You will recognize that this act of interpreting the basic idea in a work of fiction is the same that you have been performing whenever you form a central idea for any theme you write.

It should be apparent that your easiest task in determining ideas will occur when the author speaks directly. In all the other cases you must interpret indirect and dramatic statements and be alert to the implications of each work that you read. You must be certain that there is adequate justification *in the literary work* for the points that you are making about it.

THE ORGANIZATION OF YOUR THEME

In your themes, therefore, your instructor will look for the intelligence, skill, and accuracy with which you make use of the story materials as a base for your discussion of ideas. You must begin your preparation with a careful, perceptive reading of the assigned text. An idea itself usually does not require many words to express, but in order to write a good theme about it you must, in addition to naming and describing it, show how and where it is exemplified, and also demonstrate its importance in the work as a whole. The general form of your theme will probably be (a) statement of the idea, and (b) discussion of the relevance and place of the idea in the work.

Introduction

In the introduction your naming of the idea will in fact be the central idea of your theme. You should state that the idea has interest and importance in order to arouse your reader's curiosity about your paper. You might also show how you arrived at your decision to write about that particular idea. Conclude your introduction with a thesis sentence.

Body

The body of your paper should show the ways in which the writer has brought out the idea in his work. Your discussion might touch everything in the work, but in a short theme you cannot discuss everything fully. Therefore you must, as always, be selective in what you choose to discuss. Use only those details which are essential and clearly relevant.

It is easy, when you illustrate your point, to let the detail become an end in itself rather than a means toward asserting the truth of your central idea. Once you start describing the story and move away from your point, you actually have started to summarize. Remember, always, that *your central idea must always be foremost* in your reader's mind. The unifying element in your theme is this idea, and you must keep mentioning it. As you are writing, stop at various times and ask yourself: "Is this material relevant to my point so that my reader could immediately see its relevance, or is it just summary?" It is advisable to keep restating the original idea, in order to remind your reader of your purpose in writing. Everything you say should be relevant, and you must remember that your reader is not likely to be as aware of your point as you are. How can he know unless you tell him? Don't force him to do too much work, or he may stop reading your paper.

Conclusion

In your conclusion you ought to evaluate the idea and its function in the text. The evaluation of the idea is sometimes external to the text, because it may include individual attitudes (e.g., a student considering Bunyan's idea of Christian salvation in *Pilgrim's Progress* would probably

discuss his own ideas too). However, the consideration of the idea's function is artistic. How forcefully is the idea presented? How convincing is
it in the story? With answers to these questions you may conclude.

Sample Theme

The Idea of Love in D. H. Lawrence's
"The Horse Dealer's Daughter"

Lawrence demonstrates so many ideas about the love between man
and woman in this story that I cannot possibly discuss them all here.
A few separate ideas are: that love is a part of the uncontrollable side
of man's life—the emotions; that love starts with the body, and that no
satisfactory relationship between man and woman can be achieved
without this basis; that love transforms life into something new; that
love gives security since it fills an otherwise unfillable void in one's
life; that only love gives meaning to life; that love is not only something to live for, but something to be feared. Perhaps the one idea that
takes in all these is that loving is an essential part of man's nature—
that it is man's destiny to love. Lawrence's story seems to be one grand
embodiment of this basic idea. It controls the form of his story, and
all characters seem to be judged on the basis of how successfully they
live up to this idea. I will therefore discuss the idea as it appears in
what I consider to be the two main divisions of the story.

In the first part Lawrence shows us characters who are without love,
and whose lives are therefore incomplete. Thereby he illustrates the
idea that men who are not living according to their destiny will be
frustrated, cantankerous, sullen, and that they will try to find fulfillment in some other way (which will not, however, make them happy).
Their lives are virtually like those of the great draft horses, which
Lawrence describes as moving with "a massive, slumbrous strength,
and a stupidity which held them in subjection." [2] Time, Lawrence implies, is running out on people in this condition, and unless they do
something they are doomed to misery. But, according to the main idea,
an evasion of the destiny to love will not avert this doom. Joe, the oldest of the Pervin brothers, has arranged for an apparently loveless
marriage to achieve economic security. With deliberate finality, Lawrence disposes of Joe, who thereby becomes an example of the main
idea: "He would marry and go into harness. His life was over, he
would be a subject animal" (p. 178).

This idea that life virtually ends without love is finally brought to
bear upon Mabel, the lone girl in the Pervin family, and the figure for

---

2 "The Horse Dealer's Daughter," in Cleanth Brooks, John T. Purser, and Robert Penn
Warren (eds.), *An Approach to Literature,* 3rd ed. (New York: Appleton-Century-Crofts,
1952), p. 178. All page numbers refer to this edition.

whom the story is named. Just as the death of her father has precipitated the breakup of the family (who melt away at this point), the breakup is precipitating some drastic action on her part. Here the operation of Lawrence's idea is brought out clearly: since it is man's destiny to love, and since life without love is a kind of death, and since Mabel has no love on earth to anticipate but only the love for her dead father to remember, she stolidly and deliberately chooses real death with dead love, which she prefers to a life on earth without any love at all. Therefore the first section of the story closes as Mabel attempts to drown herself. She walks "toward the centre of the pond, very slowly, gradually moving deeper into the motionless water, and still moving forward as the water got up to her breast" (p. 182).

But this pond—symbolic of death as Mabel walks into it—is also a symbol of life and regeneration (for example, infant baptism employs water, and the major symbol for life in Freudian psychology is water). This generative symbolic value is dominant in the second part of Lawrence's story, and also puts into operation the second part of his idea (which has frequently been described by the old saying "Love finds a way"). Rescuing Mabel from the death to which she has consigned herself is Dr. Fergusson, who has previously been introduced as a person leading a life of quiet desperation, even though he also has derived a power from his closeness to the lives of his patients (is he living a vicarious life, or is he simply sublimating his desires?). Perhaps the good doctor's common cold, mentioned when we first meet him, is to be interpreted as a symbol of the sickness of the soul without love, and therefore the need to be well would become a strong support for Lawrence's basic idea. Whether this interpretation is right or not, however, it is important to note that Dr. Fergusson's rescue of Mabel is therapeutic not only for Mabel, but also for himself.

For the rescue follows the pattern of Lawrence's idea, and is actually a symbol of the attainment of this idea: that love rescues the life without love. But love is complex, suggests Lawrence (and in this case, it is mildly comic), and it creates new problems once it has been realized. Therefore, Lawrence builds the idea that love is something to be desired but also something to be feared. It brings out emotions that are new and strange; it violates man's naturally conservative nature; it upsets previously established equilibrium; it changes life so fundamentally that no life will ever be the same after having been touched by love. Is it any wonder that Lawrence concludes his story in the following words:

> "No, I want you, I want you," was all he answered, blindly, with that terrible intonation which frightened her almost more than the horror lest he should *not* want her.
>
> —p. 186

This complexity of emotions raises Lawrence's treatment of his idea above the level of the popular, romantic, "Hollywooden" conception of love, and answers all potential objections that love between Mabel and the doctor happens too rapidly (incidentally, Lawrence carefully demonstrates that there were emotional contacts between the two lovers before the outpouring of their love in the deserted room of the Pervin house). Lawrence's idea is mature and profound. Clearly, he suggests, love itself creates problems as great as those it solves, but it also builds a solid platform of emotional strength from which these new problems can be attacked and solved. The idea is that this strength can be achieved only when a man and woman know love, because only then are they living life as it was designed. The problems facing them then, Lawrence suggests, are the real problems that man and woman should face, since the problems are a natural result of their destiny. By contrast, the men and women without love (like those at the beginning of the story) have never reached fulfillment and consequently they face problems which, though certainly severe and immediate, are really peripheral to life as it should be lived. The entire story of Mabel and Jack, in short, is an extensive example of Lawrence's dominating idea that it is the destiny of man and woman to love.

6

The Theme of Character Analysis

*A*N EXTREMELY popular theme subject, particularly in courses in drama and novel, is the analysis of character. Though writers in ancient times wrote character sketches and novel-like stories, real interest in particularized fictional characters did not develop until the seventeenth century. In the eighteenth century the novel emerged as an important literary form. With the advent of modern psychology, interest in patterns of human behavior has come of age. Of course drama, with its centering upon a main character, has been popular since the time of the ancient Athenians. In our own times it is one of the more vital literary forms.

If you recollect some of the novels and dramas you have read or seen, you will realize that they are about characters, their reactions to an extended series of actions, and their attempts, both successful and unsuccessful, to shape those events. The novel and the drama are similar in that they show the interactions of character and action in rather full detail. To these genres one might add epic and narrative poetry, which also center upon character and action. Short stories and poems do not aim at the broadness and fullness of the larger forms, but concentrate upon only the essential high points of human experience.

WHAT IS CHARACTER?

Character in literature is a reasonable facsimile of a human being. The term is frequently applied in two senses: (a) as a reference to a personage in a work, and (b) as a reference to that personage's habits and characteristics—his total pattern of behavior. In real life we perceive a person's qualities from our contact with him. We learn about his strengths and weaknesses by observing how he speaks and acts, and, if we are on intimate terms with him, by listening to his thoughts as he communicates them to us. If we want to learn more about a particular quality, we ask him for more information about it. But in a literary work we can understand the qualities of a personage only by interpreting what the author has written about him. All the actions performed by this personage, together

41

with what he says and what is said about him, provide us with all the material from which we can make inferences about his qualities, and we can expect no more than the author has chosen to disclose. We may expect, however, that the picture presented should seem reasonably true to life (that is, the actions, statements, and thoughts of a particular personage must all be what a human being is *likely* to do, say, and think under given circumstances).

As you will immediately see, an avenue of evaluation is opened up here, for if a character does not behave as you think a true human being would behave, you have grounds for criticizing the literary work. However, your judgment on this score requires a strong imaginative boost; you must not judge simply from your own point of view, but must imagine what very different kinds of persons would do under exactly similar circumstances and with the same mental and philosophical outlooks. You can see also that this imaginative effort requires you to read the literary work sympathetically—an essential mark of a good, disciplined reader.

In studying character, then, you must look carefully at the early parts of the work in order to see what tendencies the characters have exhibited. With these characteristics in mind, you must then ask yourself "Is the subsequent action a logical consequence of this man's qualities?" In the early scenes of *Macbeth,* for example, Shakespeare demonstrates that Macbeth is a loyal, strong, valiant, and almost foolhardy warrior, that he is ambitious, but that he is also kind and gentle. In view of Macbeth's later responsibility for a series of deaths and for a brutally oppressive regime as king, the question is how to square his characteristics with the subsequent action. If it is any consolation, keep in mind that you will probably not be able to please everyone by your answer to this question, or to most questions for that matter. Ultimately, you must please yourself, and can do so if you are satisfied that your reasoning is sound throughout.

WHERE DOES CHARACTER RESIDE?

The question is an important part of the definition of *character.* The basic question is whether character is on the *inside* or on the *outside.* In other words, can a man's qualities be determined by what he says and does, or are they more truthfully determined by what he thinks and feels? And if character is inside, how can we get inside to know the character? This question is important, for example, in our consideration of men in public life, where we see the official man (his public actions and pronouncements), but have an abiding curiosity about what the man behind the official facade is like. Shakespeare, showing this sort of life in *Antony and Cleopatra,* produced one of the great plays in English because he succeeded so well in presenting materials for understanding the inner greatness of Antony and Cleopatra.

Concern for character within has permeated modern psychology, which has emphasized the inner-man concept of character so much that we may regard the action of a literary work as (a) a function of character, when the personage is sufficiently in control to determine events in the story, and (b) a series of tests by which certain qualities of a personage might be brought out when he is responding to or being shaped by events. That is, if characterization is of prime concern in the literary work, a study of that work must regard the action only as it brings out qualities of character. This view underlies many psychological novels of the twentieth century, and has been responsible for techniques like the *interior monologue* and *stream of consciousness*.

HOW IS CHARACTER DISCLOSED IN LITERATURE?

Before you prepare to write your theme, you should know the four ways in which a writer can indicate character to you:

1. By what the personage himself says (and thinks, in the third person omniscient point of view).
2. By what the character does.
3. By what other characters say about him.
4. By what the author says about him, speaking as either the storyteller or an observer of the action.

These four points require amplification.

1. What a particular character says about himself may frequently be accepted at face value for truth, but just as often it may be only a reflection of his intellectual and emotional state at a given moment. If a character in deep despair says that life is worthless, for example, you must balance that statement with what the same character says when he is happy. Then too, you must consider the situation in the literary work when a statement is made. If a character voices despair at the start, but is cheerful (or sad) at the end, there has been a development, or change, in that character's view of life. In *Crime and Punishment,* for example, Raskolnikov is convinced of his right to make judgments upon the lives of other people, but at the end of the novel he questions his right. A shift has taken place that any analysis of his qualities must consider. As you can see, you are free to interpret what a personage says in the light of the context in which it appears.

Most of the above applies to what a personage thinks as it is reported to us by the author acting as an omniscient narrator. If you detect differences between what the personage thinks and what he says, you may be sure that the author is demonstrating some quality of character, either (a) favorable, if the discrepancy is part of a worthwhile strategy, or (b) unfavorable, if the discrepancy is part of a worthless or ignoble one.

2. You have heard that what you do speaks louder than what you say. The same is true in literature, and sometimes illustrates important character traits. An author may create a character who professes honesty, yet does dishonorable things. Uriah Heep in *David Copperfield* and Tartuffe in Molière's play *Le Tartuffe* have such characteristics. Iago in *Othello* is another case in point: he professes to be Othello's friend, but secretly behaves like a devil. In analyzing what characters do, you must ask whether the character's actions are consistent with his words. If not, why not? What does the author communicate by showing inconsistencies? In the three examples just cited, the authors succeed in showing the diabolical nature of hypocrisy.

Exposing hypocrisy, however, might not be the reason for showing gaps between statement and action. This technique may illustrate ideas like "Human beings have a great capacity for self-deception," or "Human beings are weak." An author may show characters behaving consistently with what they say as a mark of favor to these characters (or also as a mark of credit to a rogue who is honest with himself, like Peachum in *The Beggar's Opera*).

3. In literature, as in life, people are always talking about other people. What they say of course raises the problem of *point of view,* because the character and motivation of a personage will condition whatever he says about someone else (see chapter 10). You know, for example, that the word of a person's enemy is usually biased against that person. Therefore an author may frequently give you a favorable impression of a character by having a bad character say bad things about him. Similarly, the word of a close friend or political manager may be biased in favor of a particular character; it must be taken with a grain of salt. In short, you must always consider the context and source of all dramatic remarks about a particular character. In Conrad's *Victory,* for example, an evil hotel manager named Schomberg always claims that the hero, Heyst, is a villain. The reader is to believe the opposite of what Schomberg says about Heyst, because Schomberg seems to be attributing his own evil motives to Heyst. By contrast, in *Macbeth,* when Macduff and Malcolm say bad things about Macbeth and his rule in Scotland, their statements should be accepted as truth because the two men are presented as honest, just, and good.

4. What the author says about a character is usually to be accepted as truth about that character. Naturally, the author must be accepted absolutely on matters of fact in the narrative or drama. But when in his own person he interprets the actions and characteristics of his characters,

he himself assumes the role of critic, and his opinions are open to question. For this reason authors frequently refrain from making overt interpretations, but devote their skill instead to arranging events in the drama
or narrative so that their own conclusions are obvious to the reader. If
the author chooses to present an analysis of character, however, he might
resort to a personage in the work who will then be bound by his own
limitations as an observer. In this case, the dramatic commentator is like
the characters discussed in 3.

COMPLETENESS OF CHARACTER DEVELOPMENT

As you study the qualities of the personage you are going to analyze,
you must consider the fullness with which he is developed. Does the
character seem to come alive, illustrating many qualities which will add
up to a really good facsimile of a human being, or does he seem to be
flat, one-sided, one-dimensional? Lola, a minor figure in Dreiser's *Sister
Carrie,* is such a character; we see little in her beyond the fact that she
is a worldly wise working girl in a chorus line. She is not fully realized.
Stephen Dedalus, the major figure in *A Portrait of the Artist as a Young
Man,* on the other hand, is fully realized, because his thoughts, words,
responses, and actions are described fully from earliest consciousness to
young adulthood. The degree to which an author can make a character
come alive is a mark of his skill; if you think that your author is successful in this regard, you should say so in your theme.

THE ORGANIZATION OF YOUR THEME

Introduction

As always, your theme should have a clearly stated central idea that
runs throughout your entire character analysis. Your central idea here
will be whatever general statement you make to describe the character
you analyze. Your thesis sentence must be a brief statement of the main
sections of the body of your theme.

Body

Your organization is designed to illustrate and prove your central idea.
You have much freedom in organizing your main points. Some possible
methods are the following:

1. Organization around central characteristics, like "kindness, gentle-
ness, generosity, firmness," or "resoluteness of will frustrated by inoppor-
tune moments for action, resulting in despondency, doubt, and melan-

choly." A body containing this sort of material would demonstrate how the literary work brings out each of these qualities.

2. Organization around central incidents that reveal primary characteristics (see, for example, the sample theme). Certain key incidents will stand out in a work, and you might create an effective body by using three or four of these as guides for your discussion, taking care to show in your topic sentences that your purpose in this arrangement is to illuminate the character you have selected, not the incidents. In other words, you would regard the incidents only as they bring out truths about character. In a discussion of the character of Stephen in *A Portrait of the Artist as a Young Man,* an effective arrangement might be to select the incidents of the pandybat, the prostitute, and the young girl standing in the water.

Naturally, with this arrangement, you would have to show how the incidents bring out the characteristics, and also how they serve to explain other things the character might do.

3. Organization around various sections of the work. This arrangement is particularly effective if you are demonstrating that a character is undergoing changes and developments. In analyzing the character of Iago, for example, you might say that up to Act II, Scene iii of *Othello* he behaves in a reasonably motivated way, that from there to Act V he behaves like a devil, and that in Act V he becomes an enigma.

Conclusion

The conclusion should contain your statements about how the characteristics you have brought out are related to the work as a whole. If the personage was good but came to a bad end, does this discrepancy elevate him to tragic stature? If he was a nobody and came to a bad end, does this fact cause you to draw any conclusion about the class or type of which he was a part? Or does it illustrate the author's view of human life? Or both? Do the characteristics explain why the personage helps or hinders other characters in the literary work? Does your analysis help you to clear up any misunderstanding that your first reading of the work produced? Questions like these should be raised and answered in your conclusion.

A WARNING ABOUT DICTION

In view of the closeness between character analysis and psychology, you must realize that for a literary theme it is best to avoid technical terms from psychology. Even if you have acquired much skill in using these terms, your instructor will probably not receive them sympathetically if you substitute them for thoughtful analysis. Always explain yourself, and do not descend to jargon, as there is great danger of doing in this theme.

Some words from psychology are admissible, however, without much amplification: words like *disturbed, frustrated, anxiety* are satisfactory because they are in common use, but if you start using words like *complex, neurosis,* and *psychosis,* you should explain the concepts, not just use the words. Be cautious, and use common sense. If you have any question about a word, ask your instructor.

Sample Theme

The Character of Jim in Conrad's Lord Jim

Jim is hard to understand. He is seen mainly through the eyes of Marlow, who imparts his own values to much of the story. He also is the subject of much interpretation by other informants in the story, so that we receive many views of him. In addition, Jim is the principal figure in a richly symbolic tapestry, so that much of what he does and says is relevant to most people at most times. In this respect his individuality is sacrificed to his existence as a symbol. Despite these difficulties, however, Jim emerges as a fully developed individual, even though we do not hear of every detail that might ever have concerned him. To me, the key to understanding Jim's character is that he is a man capable of imagining the best in himself and in men generally—a man whose action at any given moment is controlled by an idea of the best. He is, in Stein's word, a "romantic," and I would add that he is an introspective dreamer. I believe that his character is made clear by three incidents in the novel, all of which are connected with leaps, or jumps, that Jim either makes or does not make.

When Jim has his first opportunity to leap, he does not take it. This failure to jump is symbolic of Jim's preference for mental over physical heroism. It hurts his own high evaluation of himself. Imbued with the British ideals of manhood and adventure in the days of the naval empire, he has been dreaming of his own "devotion to duty" in a way "as unflinching as a hero in a book." [1] But when the opportunity comes to join in a rescue operation, he misses the boat. He does not jump. From this point Jim becomes a drifter, for this failure has given him a hint of the basic indecision (*cowardice* would be too strong a word at this point) which is worrying the bubble of his own self esteem. This one incident, in short, explains the moral laziness which finally causes him to ship aboard the *Patna.*

The bubble of Jim's esteem is totally destroyed by his second jump —from the *Patna* when it is listing heavily and supposedly near sinking. This jump is the major incident in the novel, since it brings out the depths of Jim's being, that inner panic which destroys all his conscious dreams by causing a single cowardly act despite his good intentions.

[1] Joseph Conrad, *Lord Jim* (New York: The Modern Library, 1931), p. 6.

This jump brings out Jim's sense of shame, which must be overwhelming, since it causes him to wander all over the Indian Ocean, fleeing whenever anybody mentions the *Patna* episode. With his depths thus exposed, I believe that Jim feels morally naked, without the privacy that most of us have, since we know, or hope, that the depths of our own souls may never emerge to haunt us. Jim's emerges, and he runs from it, as run he must.

But the *Patna* jump also emphasizes Jim's good qualities. He has a high sense of justice, and before he runs he therefore faces trial, which can end in nothing but his dishonor and disgrace. His conscious dream of what is right has enabled him to face the consequences of his real guilt. Perhaps this facing of the trial when all the other deserters flee is the start of Jim's awareness, acted upon but never clearly stated by him, that life constantly demands expiation for guilt that is caused not entirely by our own choice.

Jim's final leap results from his own choice, however, and as such it enables him finally to live out his dream. It is a kind of triumph. Leaping over the fence enclosing Rajah Allang's courtyard, he allies himself with Doramin, and proceeds quickly to justify the title *Lord Jim* by acting wisely, in concert with Doramin, in governing the forlorn outpost of Patusan. He is convinced of the value of his dream, and always behaves with justice, honor, and firmness, yet always with forgiveness. These are the conscious virtues, to which Jim adheres closely, since they are the embodiment of his character as a dreamer.

This adherence explains why he accepts the final responsibility for the death of Dain Waris. Beyond question, his third leap has enabled him to dedicate himself to the good life in Patusan as expiation for his guilt in the *Patna* episode. The personal quality of this dedication should be stressed, however, and contrasted with the quality of Jim's feelings after Gentleman Brown commits his treacherous act. In this affair Jim is responsible only for not having destroyed the Gentleman *before* the murder is committed. Yet, in Gentleman Brown, Jim apparently sees that the cowardly depths are common to all mankind, not just to himself. So Jim faces Doramin in expiation, just as he had earlier braved the court and the subsequent disgrace. But as Jim sacrifices himself, the best in him, his capacity to dream, triumphs over whatever it was that made him leap from the *Patna*. He is genuinely great at that moment of sacrifice, when he expiates for us all, as it were.

Admittedly, Jim is a puzzling character, since his characteristics show that human life is a mystery and since we never really get inside him. But Conrad uses him to demonstrate that, if life has its depths, it also has its high points. At the highest point, a human being willing to live out his dream, if this dream has value and ennobles mankind, can justify the claim that life is elevated and great. Jim, with all his frailty, is a truly great representation of a human being, since he has met and conquered life's greatest obstacle—the deflation of one's own high self-esteem.

7

The Comparison-Contrast Theme

A POPULAR theme subject is the comparison of different authors, of two or more works by the same author, of different drafts of the same work, or of different characters, incidents, and ideas within the same work or in different works. Your instructor may assign this theme in many ways, such as "Compare X and Y," or "Discuss the idea of Z in such-and-such works." No matter how the assignment is made, your job is to write a comparison-contrast theme. This assignment requires a detailed study and a thorough consideration of a much wider range of material than is needed to write a theme about a single work, idea, character, or author.

COMPARISON-CONTRAST AS A WAY TO KNOWLEDGE

Comparison and contrast are important means to the gaining of understanding. If you have ever looked at your hands together, for example, you probably just saw two hands, but if you put your hands next to someone else's, you quickly were able to see salient characteristics of your own simply because of the contrast. You realized that hands are hands, with all their identical qualities, but you also perceived differences between yours and the other person's. In short, similarities between things are brought out by *comparison,* and differences are brought out by *contrast.* The essences of objects and artistic works can be quickly illustrated by use of the comparison-contrast method.

You will quickly perceive that the comparison-contrast method is closely related to the study of *definition,* because definition aims at the description of a particular thing by identifying its properties while also isolating it from everything else. Comparison-contrast is also closely allied with Plato's idea that we learn a thing best by reference to its opposite; that is, one way of finding out what a thing *is* is to find out what it is *not.*

In your literature courses, your use of comparison-contrast will therefore enable you to define and describe the particular characteristics of a particular writer or work by showing the general category to which your subject belongs and also by differentiating it from all other members of the category. Another way of thinking of a comparison-contrast assignment is to regard it in the same way that a jeweler regards a fine jewel, which can be made more beautiful if put into a fine setting. To a great degree, the method of comparison-contrast can be used to set off a great literary work by comparison with inferior works. In these senses, this type of theme is an integral part of literary classification, literary history (because it takes time differences into account), and literary evaluation (it implies that along with separation goes the cause for separation, including the rating of works and authors into orders of superiority and inferiority). When your instructor asks you to "Compare Pope and Tennyson," or to "Compare and contrast Chaucer with Edgar Guest," you should realize that he is asking you to bring out some of the important points that make the study of literature a true discipline.

INTENTION AND PREPARATION

Do not begin to write this, or any theme, without a plan or intention. Your first problem is to decide your objective. You ought to relate the material of the assignment to the purposes of the course, for the comparison-contrast method can be focused upon a number of points. One focal point may simply be the equal and mutual illumination of both (or more) subjects of comparison; thus, in a survey course, where your purpose is to gain a general understanding of all the writers in the course, a theme about Milton and Pope would serve to describe the methods of both poets without throwing primary attention upon either. But suppose you are taking a course in Milton—then your comparison-contrast theme could use Pope's methods as a means of highlighting Milton's; your theme would finally be about Milton, and your discussion of Pope would be relevant only as it related to this purpose. Conversely, if you were taking a course in eighteenth-century literature, you might use a discussion of Milton only as it illuminated Pope, and your theme would ultimately be about Pope. You will see that your first task is therefore to decide where to place your emphasis, because comparison-contrast may be used for both purposes described in this paragraph. In the sample theme, the writer has compared two poems by Donne and Wordsworth, and his rhetorical purpose is to demonstrate Donne's superiority. Thus the sample theme is actually about Donne.

Your second problem is to select the proper material—the grounds of your discussion. It is useless to compare essentially dissimilar things, for then your basic conclusions will be of limited value. Therefore your task is to put the works or writers you are comparing onto common ground. Compare like with like; i.e., style with style, subject with subject, idea with idea, structure with structure, characterization with characterization, prosody with prosody, milieu with milieu, evaluation with evaluation, and so on. Putting your subjects onto common ground makes you arrive at a reasonable basis of comparison and therefore a legitimate occasion for contrast. Nothing can be learned, for example, from a comparison of "Pope's style and Milton's philosophy." But much can be learned from a comparison of "the influence of philosophy upon style in Milton and Pope." The first promises little, while the second suggests common ground, with points of both comparison and divergence and with further implications about the ages in which the two poets lived.

In attempting to find common ground, seek possible similarities as you prepare yourself by reading and taking notes for the assignment. Here your generalizing powers will assist you, for apparently dissimilar materials may meet—if you are able to perceive the meeting place. Thus a comparison of *The House of Mirth* by Edith Wharton and *The Catcher in the Rye* by J. D. Salinger might put the works onto the common ground of "The Treatment of the 'Outsider,'" or "Corrosive Influences of an Affluent Society upon the Individual," or "The Basis of Social Criticism," even though the works are about different characters living in different ages. As you can see, what appears at first dissimilar can often be put into a frame of reference that permits analytical comparison and contrast. Much of your success in writing will depend upon your ingenuity in finding a suitable basis for comparison.

METHODS OF COMPARISON

Let us assume that you have decided upon your rhetorical purpose and upon the basis or bases of your comparison: you have done your reading, taken your notes, and know what you want to say. The remaining problem is the treatment of your material. Here are two acceptable ways.

A common, but inferior, way is to make your points first about one work and then to do the same for the other. This method makes your paper seem like two big lumps, and it also involves much repetition, because you must repeat the same points as you treat your second subject. This first method, in other words, is only satisfactory—it is no better than a C method.

The superior method is to treat your main idea in its major aspects, and to make references to the two (or more) writers as the reference illustrates and illuminates your main idea. Thus you would be constantly referring to both writers, sometimes within the same sentence, and would be reminding your reader of the point of your discussion. There are reasons for the superiority of the second method: (a) you do not need to repeat your points unnecessarily, for you can document them as you raise them; (b) by referring to the two writers in relatively close juxtaposition

in relation to a clearly stated basis of comparison, you can avoid making
a reader with a poor memory reread previous sections. Frequently such
readers do not bother to reread, and as a result they are never really clear
about what you have said. As a good example, however, here is a paragraph from a student theme on "Nature as a basis of comparison in
William Wordsworth's 'The World Is Too Much with Us' and Gerard
Manley Hopkin's 'God's Grandeur.'" The virtue of the paragraph is
that it uses material from both poets as a means of development; the
material is synthesized by the student:

> 1 Hopkins's ideas are Christian, though not genuinely other-worldly.
> 2 God is a God of the world for Hopkins, and "broods with warm breast
> and with ah! bright wings" (1.14); Hopkins is convinced that God is here
> and everywhere, for his first line triumphantly proclaims this. 3 Words-
> worth, by contrast, is able to perceive the beauty of Nature, but feels that
> God in the Christian sense has deserted him. 4 Wordsworth is to be de-
> fended here, though, because his wish to see Proteus or to hear Triton is
> not pagan. 5 He wants, instead, to have faith, to have the conviction that
> Hopkins so confidently claims. 6 Even if the faith is pagan, Wordsworth
> would like it just so he could have firm, unshakable faith. 7 As a matter
> of fact, however, Wordsworth's perception of Nature gives the contradic-
> tion to the lack of faith he claims. 8 His God is really Nature itself. 9
> Hopkins's more abstract views of Nature make me feel that the Catholic
> believes that Nature is only a means to the worship of God. 10 For Hop-
> kins, God is supreme; for Wordsworth, Nature is.

If H and W are allowed to stand for ideas about Hopkins and Wordsworth, the paragraph may be schematized as follows:

> (Each number stands for a sentence number.)
> $1 = H.$ $2 = H.$ $3 = W.$ $4 = W.$ $5 = W, H.$ $6 = W.$
> $7 = W.$ $8 = W.$ $9 = H.$ $10 = H, W.$

This interweaving of subject material (two of the sentences contain references to both poets) gives the impression that the student has learned both
poems so well that he is able to think of them together. Mental "digestion" has taken place. When the student discusses Hopkins's idea of Nature, he is able to think of it immediately in relation to Wordsworth's,
and brings out references to both poets as he writes. You can profit from
his example. If you can develop your comparison-contrast theme in this
interlocking way, you will write it more economically and clearly than
you would by the first method (this statement is true of tests as well as
themes). Beyond that, if you have actually digested the material as successfully as the interlocking method shows, you will be demonstrating
that you have fulfilled one of the primary goals of education—the assimila-
tion and *use* of material.

THE ORGANIZATION OF YOUR THEME

First you must narrow your subject into a topic you can handle conveniently within the limits of the assignment. If you have been assigned a comparison of Tennyson and Pope, for example, pick out one or two poems of each poet, and write your theme about them. You must be wary, however, of the limitations of this selection: generalizations made from one or two works may not apply to the broad subject originally proposed. If you state this qualification somewhere in your theme, however, your comparison will have much value, and your instructor will probably be pleased with the wisdom of your selection.

Introduction

State what works, authors, characters, and ideas are under consideration, then show how you have narrowed the basis of your comparison. Your central idea will be a brief statement of what can be learned from your paper: the general similarities and differences which you have observed from your comparison and/or the superiority of one work or author over another. Your thesis sentence should anticipate the body of your theme.

Body

The body of your theme depends upon the points you have chosen for comparison. You might be comparing two works on the basis of *structure, tone, style,* two authors on *ideas,* or two characters on *character traits.* In your discussion you would necessarily use the same methods that you would use in writing a theme about these terms in a single work, except that here (a) you are exemplifying your points by reference to more subjects than one, and (b) your ultimate rhetorical purpose is the illumination of the subjects upon which your comparison is based; in this sense, the methods you use in talking about *structure* or *style* are not "pure," but are instead subordinate to your aims of comparison-contrast. Let us say, for example, that you are comparing the ideas in two different works. The first part of your theme might be devoted to the analysis of and description of the similarities and dissimilarities of the ideas *as* ideas. Your interest here is not so much to explicate the ideas of either work separately as to explicate the ideas of both works in order to show points of agreement and disagreement. A second part might be given over to the influences of the ideas upon the *structure* and *style* of the particular works; that is, how the ideas help make the works similar or dissimilar. Or, let us say that your subjects of comparison are two or more characters.

Your points might be to show similarities and dissimilarities of mental
and spiritual qualities, and of activities in which the characters engage.

Conclusion

In this section you should bring out the conclusions that your study
has caused to emerge. If your writers were part of a "school" or "period,"
you might show how your findings relate to these larger movements. You
ought also to illustrate the limitations and implications of your treatment;
you might show that more could be done along the same lines, and what
might be the effects of pursuing the method further.

Sample Theme

The Use of *Westward*
In Wordsworth's "Stepping Westward" and in
Donne's "Good Friday, 1613, Riding Westward" [1]

The reason for comparing these two poems is obvious from the
titles, and the similarities become more obvious as a person reads the
poems. Both employ "westward" as the direction in which the speakers move. As they move, they become aware of death, since the west—
where the sun sets and the day dies—is the traditional direction sym-
bolizing death. The reality of this situation causes the speakers to
meditate upon religion and philosophy. There is a difference in the
ways in which the speakers move. Wordsworth's speaker is *stepping*
westward, while Donne's is *riding* (i.e., being carried). If these actions
can be interpreted symbolically, Wordsworth may be suggesting that
his speaker's will is governing him, while Donne may be suggesting
that his speaker's will is subordinate to something external. The poems
tend to bear out this distinction. My feeling is that the differences in
these poems are more noteworthy than the similarities, and that
Donne's poem emerges as better, more forceful, and more realistic than
Wordsworth's. This superiority can be seen clearly in the ideas that
both poets have about the forces that govern life.

The idea of moving westward prompts both poets to be concerned
with the nature of life once the fact of death has been taken into account. Death is, in other words, the one unavoidable fact that causes
everyone to pause and think. On the nature of life, Wordsworth seems

---

1 Quotations from "Good Friday, 1613" are taken from *The Complete Poetry and
Selected Prose of John Donne & The Complete Poetry of William Blake,* with an intro-
duction by Robert Silliman Hillyer (New York: Random House, Inc., 1946), pp. 247-248.
Quotations from "Stepping Westward" are taken from *The Complete Poetical Works of
Wordsworth,* Andrew J. George, ed. (Cambridge, Mass.: Houghton Mifflin Co., 1932),
p. 298.

to be raising a question that Donne has already answered. Wordsworth's poem asks whether we are governed by chance—the *"wildish destiny"*—or whether we are controlled by *"heavenly"* forces. Naturally, he opts for the "heavenly" destiny to guide him on his "endless way." Donne does not raise this question, however, for there is no doubt in his mind that the heavenly destiny exists; his idea, instead, is that his speaker is riding *away* from his destiny, since God is in the East, and "Pleasure" and "businesse" are whirling his "Soule," like a "Spheare" westward away from God. On a nonparadoxical level, Donne uses this opposition of East and West to bring out a conflict between faith and human frailty—a conflict that is far different from the relative calm in Wordsworth's poem.

Donne's poem is not only more agitated than Wordsworth's, but it contains images which demonstrate that Donne is out after bigger game than Wordsworth. The first image is described by the sentence "Let mans Soule be a Spheare." The individual soul, from this image, is a world in itself over which the forces of good and evil contend, and the loss of any individual is of cosmic significance to God. I have sought unsuccessfully for anything of comparable imaginative force in Wordsworth's poem. Donne's other image is that of Christ on the Cross, a symbol at once of both death and life, who, in Donne's paradoxical expression, by dying made death an entry way into life. The westward direction of travel therefore becomes not only the direction of death, but also of life—heavenly life—since it ultimately is the direction in which one must travel in order to see God:

> Hence is't, that I am carryed towards the West
> This day, when my Soules forme bends towards the East.
> There I should see a Sunne, by rising set,
> And by that setting endlesse day beget;
> But that Christ on this Crosse, did rise and fall,
> Sinne had eternally benighted all.
>
> —lines 9–14

This short passage, ending with the word *all*, demonstrates that man's soul is in the balance. The conflict is thus not just personal, it is typical of all men. On the one hand they see the good, but on the other they do not follow it, and so the conflict is cosmic. But as they avoid God, they move toward death, which is another, and more permanent, way to God.

Donne's world, in short, is much more complex and difficult than Wordsworth's. I do not imply that Wordsworth interprets life as easy, for "In a strange Land and far from home" his speaker feels that "The dewy ground was dark and cold; / Behind, all gloomy to behold;" (4, 9, 10). But Wordsworth simply does not imply anything like Donne's force. As a result, after Wordsworth's speaker decides that his destiny is "heavenly," the dark, dewy ground is transformed into a "region bright" (16). This change strikes me as a little too simple, a little too pat. By contrast, Donne's world (the soul) is constantly "Subject to forraigne motions," which drive it away from its heavenly destiny, corroding it and deforming it. His speaker therefore ends the poem in anguished prayer, asking God to purify his life so that he can withstand death:

> O thinke mee worth thine anger, punish mee,
> Burne off my rusts, and my deformity,
> Restore thine Image, so much, by thy grace,
> That thou may'st know mee, and I'll turne my face.
>
> —lines 39–42

Thus, for Donne, the only salvation in this difficult life is God's love, which enabled endurance upon the Cross, where His flesh was "rag'd and torne" (28). Paradoxically again, God dying on the Cross is a sight upon which the speaker "durst not looke"; consequently his ride westward is an almost inevitable result of his own weakness, for which God is the only remedy. These are contorted, tortuous ideas, which are sharply in contrast with Wordsworth's emphasis upon "human sweetness" and "The very sound of courtesy." Both ideas are in accord so far as they account for the individual's dependency for support upon something external, but Donne's thought is full of pain, uncertainty, anguish, and paradox, while Wordsworth's is characterized by calm, certainty, and simplicity.

The principal difference between the two poems is, I think, that Donne's view of life is fuller, rounder than Wordsworth's. Wordsworth's problem ends where Donne's starts. This difference is perhaps the same one that exists between a fairy tale ending on the note that "They lived happily ever after," and a modern novel that treats the problems and anguish that frequently appear in adult life. This difference applies only to these two poems, for Wordsworth brings out personal conflicts elsewhere: poems like The Prelude, the "Ode to Duty," and the "Immortality" ode illustrate that life, to him, was not pure unruffled calm. (Nor does he, presumably, have in his poem the idea of the Crucifixion before him, as Donne of course did on Good Friday.) But even in these poems one does not find a view of life comparable in violence to what Donne shows in his poem about the errant soul's westward departure from God hanging "upon the tree" (36).

8

The Theme on a Literary Work as It Reflects Its Historical Period

*E*VERYTHING written, spoken, painted, or composed reflects to some degree the period of its composition. Indeed, we cannot open our mouths without showing attitudes, idioms, and customs of our time and place. Everything belongs in its historical period, whether as a revolutionary idea, reaction, or synthesis, and the job of the literary historian is to define and describe the historical movements in which the various artistic works belong. This theme will help you understand the relationship of literature to history, and, although you are not expected to write literary history, you will perhaps see how literary history comes about.

Though most literary artists aim at universality, they are also men of their time, and most of their subjects are contemporary. There is a mild critical problem here, for some writers begin with a "universal" view, which they exemplify by their work, while others profess to begin only with their subject material, and say nothing about whether their works are "universal." Let us for the nonce regard this question also as a matter of history, however, for whatever method the writer espouses, his work must be of general or "universal" significance if it is to survive its own period. Your immediate concern as you read the assigned work for this theme is to observe the effects of the time of composition on the work. To make your observations you should regard such things as style, ideas, structure of the work, culture traits and artifacts described in the work (thus a work written in 1880 about life on the frontier will probably mention such things as axes, rifles, wood stoves, and Saturday-night baths). Also consider the occupations of the characters, the ideal types of characters (the types the writer asks you to admire), the types of villains (whom the writer asks you to reject), and the assumptions held by various characters. These qualities and many others date the compositions in which they appear. Some historical knowledge is necessary if you are to place the work properly in its time. In judging a work of nineteenth-century fiction, for example, you should not raise, as a student once did, the question of why the characters in the work did not attend movies or watch television.

In analyzing the work assigned, you must of course limit the problem you will undertake to solve and the aspects of the work that you will consider. Let us suppose that your topic is "The Problems of the Lower Classes at the Turn of the Century as seen in Dreiser's *Sister Carrie.*" This theme would probably focus upon the early experiences of Carrie at her sister's and at the factory, the causes leading to her relationships with Drouet and Hurstwood, and Hurstwood's miseries during his decline. The theme would touch upon job conditions, poverty, cost of living, and the characters' reactions to these conditions, together with Dreiser's opinions on the subject. Similarly, a theme about "Home Life in Dublin as Shown in *A Portrait of the Artist as a Young Man*" would be concerned with characterizations of the family, with the preoccupations of Mr. Dedalus with politics and religion, with Stephen's reactions to these and other concerns, and with many other happenings in the Dedalus home. Or you might treat the topic of "The Age of Experimentation in Literature as Illustrated by the Structure of *A Portrait of the Artist as a Young Man.*"

You can see that many of the techniques already learned will be useful for this theme; you will, however, have to direct your reading—and your note-taking on the reading—toward providing material and approaches for this particular topic.

This theme will help you to understand the making of literary history. It shows that literature is a part of history, and a valuable part. Whereas history is concerned with general actions of a society, literature presents specific examples of people living in that society, and records their problems, their ways of meeting them, their failures, their successes, and their dreams. The theme will also make you a better reader, because it will acquaint you with those elements in a literary work that are dated—perpetually a part of their time—and will enable you to distinguish these elements from those which are "universal"—for all times. And this topic will open up another avenue of evaluation, which you may enter by asking and answering these questions: "To what extent has history bypassed the problems delineated in this work? Are the problems like those still facing people today? Do the solutions to these problems have possible value to us today? To people in the future?" In short, as the historical events in the work take on similarity to your own problems and to what you perceive as basic human problems, the work acquires vitality, and may receive your favorable judgment.

You should enjoy writing this theme. Your curiosity about how people of other places and times behaved and thought should be satisfied when you approach a literary work in this way.

THE ORGANIZATION OF YOUR THEME

The form of your theme should permit you to announce and limit your subject, to examine the historical data in a coherent way, and to arrive at general conclusions about the work.

Introduction

Your introduction should discuss briefly the period in which the work was written and the relationship of the work to that period. In a discussion of *Sister Carrie,* for example, you would mention the date of publication (1900) and the period of time covered by the novel (c. 1887– c. 1900). Then you would probably state that Chicago and New York were neither as populous nor as developed as they are now, and that growing industrialism was creating problems between labor and management. Then, of course, you would present your thesis sentence.

Body

The body of the paper should steadfastly pursue your point. Here you may want to bring several different approaches to bear upon your topic. You may refer to the author's style, the structure of his book, his leading ideas, his preconceptions, the events in the book, as well as the clothing styles, machinery, speech habits, topics of conversation, and habits of thought of the characters. In short, your point in this section may be illuminated by many different techniques for describing literature. Throughout the section, however, you should remember that these approaches are not ends in themselves, but are useful only as they help you to illustrate the relationship between the work under discussion and its historical period.

Conclusion

You here evaluate the work according to its success in giving a picture of life at a particular period. To what extent has the author dealt with the issues of his time? Has he chosen to ignore them, and if so, why? You should also attempt to discuss how well the writer makes the problems of his time universal; in other words, is the work interesting and important to us today? Do you think it will be of importance to people of the future? In answering these questions, you will be evaluating the work you have analyzed.

Sample Theme

The Concerns of a Literate Conservative in the Days of Charles II, as Shown in Dryden's Poem "The Medal, a Satire Against Sedition" (1683)

Dryden published "The Medal" in March, 1683, almost four months after the Earl of Shaftesbury (the Whig who, with the Duke of Monmouth, Charles II's "natural" son, had engineered the proposed coup against Charles II) had been acquitted of treason charges brought by Charles and his followers. Since Dryden's "Absalom and Achitophel" (1682), written before the acquittal, had dealt with his belief that Shaftesbury was politically dangerous, and "The Medal" dealt with the new dangers posed, in Dryden's opinion, by Shaftesbury after the acquittal, the two poems are actually companion pieces, treating the same subject in different ways. Both poems bring out extended arguments against insurrection, and both bring out the concerns of men of the age with classical and Biblical themes and with partisan politics. While "Absalom and Achitophel" is an elevated satire, written as an epic poem, "The Medal" is a direct outcry in which the emotions of indignation and rage are fully apparent. "Absalom and Achitophel" is kind, as satires go, but "The Medal" is cruel and biting. As a historical document, the style and subject matter of "The Medal" combine to show how an intelligent, conservative, literate Tory who was also a poet responded to an issue which had gone against him. History tells us that Shaftesbury was acquitted. "The Medal" shows us an attack that, while ineffective in arousing opinion against him, must have pleased many of his Tory opponents.

In carrying out his attack, Dryden demonstrated concern for the techniques of satire, concern which actually shows us a great deal about the minds of his readers, or at least about his estimation of these minds. First of all, the poem is an invective; that is, it attacks Shaftesbury and his followers directly, by means principally of insults. But a number of assumptions underlie this invective. Since from Dryden's point of view the situation was one in which an unjust side had misused law for its own disruptive ends, he had grounds for "indignation" as defined and described by Aristotle in the *Rhetoric* (II, 9). Certainly Dryden did not need a classical precedent for every method he used, but it is true that an indignant writer will naturally try to arouse anger and fear in his readers, rather than seek to amuse them with gentle irony. As a result, Dryden in "The Medal" found the satiric techniques of the classical Roman poet Persius completely germane to his purposes. I submit that Dryden's attack upon Shaftesbury and his followers on the grounds that they were literally insane and monstrously repulsive would have been understood by his more literate contemporaries as being in the tradition of classical satire in the style of Persius. In truth, the poem shows the extremity of feeling usually associated with Persius, an extremity that Dryden embodies in his outcry "Help, Heaven!" (line 137).[1]

The atmosphere of the poem thus reflects knowledge of a certain mode of classical satire; the subject material, too, is related to a conservative point of view that is rooted in the classical, Platonic, distrust and hatred of democracy. As Dryden uses the word *democracy*, he means mob rule, the sense in which Plato usually speaks about it. The structure of the poem always moves from the specific—e.g., the early reference to the medal and Shaftesbury—to the general—e.g., the Whig followers of Shaftesbury, the mob. The mob is shown to respond readily to the demagogue's persuasiveness; they follow false schemes, which lead ultimately to the destruction of all orderly principles of government, and therefore to anarchy. The mob is an unmanageable force which, once turned loose, cannot be governed or checked, deserving only of scorn and hatred:

> Those [i.e., the fool and knave, the constituents
> of the mob] let me curse; what vengeance will they urge,
> Whose ordures neither plague nor fire can purge. . . .
> —lines 187–188

Dryden expresses his scorn in his control of his lines. While the pattern is heroic couplets, there are many triplets in this poem, indicating that the mob is as swollen as the lines. In one case Dryden even wrote a fourteen-syllable line, to indicate their bursting out of bounds. Let us observe this passage in context:

> Almighty crowd, thou shorten'st all dispute;
> Pow'r is thy essence, wit thy attribute!
> Nor faith nor reason make thee at a stay,
> Thou leap'st o'er all eternal truths in thy Pindaric way!
> —lines 91–94

Dryden brings out the moderate Toryism underlying his attack upon mob rule in the lines in which he attacks the "impious axioms" (i.e., democratic principles) of the commonwealth. (It must be emphasized that these principles were to be identified with the dissenting religious position):

> Such impious axioms foolishly they show,
> For in some soils republics will not grow:
> Our temp'rate isle will no extremes sustain

---

1 *The Poetical Works of Dryden* (rev. ed.), George R. Noyes, ed. (Cambridge, Mass.: Houghton Mifflin Co., 1950), p. 129. All line numbers refer to this edition.

Of pop'lar sway or arbitrary reign,
But slides between them both into the best,
Secure in freedom, in a monarch blest;
And tho' the climate, vex'd with various winds,
Works thro' our yielding bodies on our minds,
The wholesome tempest purges what it breeds,
To recommend the calmness that succeeds.

—lines 246–255

While the poem thus demonstrates the conservative and royalist-Tory position upon mob rule at the immediate time of the poem, it also prophesies what will happen if the mob is allowed to go its own way in the future. Dryden relied upon the literacy of his audience when he referred to the "Canaanite" in the land of England (line 178). This Biblical reference leads to a more extended allusion to the Naboth vineyard episode of the Old Testament (I Kings 21). The fact that the Bible tells of Elijah's presence in Israel at the time Ahab and Jezebel usurped Naboth's vineyard, together with the fact that Elijah pronounced doom upon Ahab for the crime (I Kings 21:20–24), leads to Dryden's predictions at the end of "The Medal," much in the vein of Biblical prophecy:

And frogs and toads, and all the tadpole train,
Will croak to Heav'n for help from this devouring crane.
The cutthroat sword and clamorous gown shall jar,
In sharing their ill-gotten spoils of war:
Chiefs shall be grudg'd the part which they pretend;
Lords envy lords, and friends with every friend
About their impious merit shall contend.
The surly commons shall respect deny,
And justle peerage out with property. . . .

—lines 304–12

In its attack upon democracy, the poem may be displeasing to us today, because human experience since Dryden's time has shown that with the increasing, if imperfect, literacy accompanying the advent of the mass man, the only practicable form of government is democracy. Before dismissing Dryden's views as being merely dated, however, we should realize that to him government's most desirable function was to provide stability; in Dryden's experience, democracy was literally anarchy. In our experience, democracy has been stable only when it has adhered to the principles Dryden desired—namely, respect for law and stability, with needed reforms to be gained usually through due process of law rather than through revolution. To the extent that Dryden did not envisage that democracy could evolve this respect for law, his poem is dated, but in his concern for law and order his work is remarkably timely, and, I believe, universal. Dryden's concern with the styles of satire is today, regrettably, of mainly historical interest, even though most of us can recognize the difference between satire that attacks by direct invective, on the one hand, and that which attacks by indirect irony and humor, on the other. Dryden's Biblical allusions are perhaps at once the most dated and the most universal and timely aspects of his poem: by suggesting that the effects caused by the violation of law and order in Biblical times were like the effects in his own time, Dryden's poem suggests that the parallel would also work for our times, and for future times. One needs only to regard the current spectacles in the world to observe that the material of Dryden's poem is of more than passing significance. The poem is an outstanding example of the way in which a superb literary craftsman can raise a topical issue into an issue of universal human importance.

9

The Theme on Imagery in a Literary Work

IMAGERY originally applied to words standing for things that could be seen, but at present it is applied loosely to words representing things that can be perceived by any of the five senses. When you hear the word *imagery*, therefore, it refers to words that can cause an imaginative response from sight, smell, taste, touch, or hearing. A theme about imagery will be about these words, the sense impressions they convey, and their importance in the work. Most often you will be asked to analyze the imagery in a poem. However, prose is also filled with images, and you might write a good theme analyzing imagery in a work of prose.

The rationale of imagery is that your sense impressions are recorded ("impressed") in your memory as a series of images, or pictures. At one time, in fact, the words *imagination* and *memory* meant the same: a storehouse for images. In the processes of speech and writing, your memory supplies you with mental pictures selected from your past sense impressions, and as you express yourself, you describe these pictures. Your words depend upon what your mind's eye can see, as though you were re-experiencing and describing at the same moment images that have been stored in your memory. Directly related to this idea of composition is the term, *imaginative literature,* which means literature that has been created largely from the memory or imagination (a broad term for the creative processes of the mind) of the writer, as distinguished from biography, or history, which are dependent upon factual sources outside the writer's mind and are less subject to the writer's creative processes. If you have ever spoken these words about someone—"He has a strong (or vivid) imagination"—you were describing a quality that is closely related to imaginative literature. What you probably meant is that the person has a propensity for supposing things that are beyond immediate reality. But if you were to find a person who combined this tendency with the abilities to describe vividly his impressions or series of impressions, to put together a combination of impressions forcefully, originally, or unusually, and to make these impressions relevant to a specific situation, you would have found a good storyteller or even a good writer.

When you read, you attempt to reverse the process of imaginative creation in order to re-experience images like those originally in the mind of the writer. In this sense, reading is really a creative experience. You see the words on the page and they actively stimulate you to re-create something akin to what the author himself perceived, though this duplication cannot ever be exact. Words must remain on the page, and images can be perceived only in the mind. *Imagery* refers to the process by which words stimulate images.

In writing a theme about imagery, then, you are dealing with one of the ways in which the quality of a writer shows. You are considering how well, how vividly, he has been able to transfer, by words only, the impressions from his own mind to yours.

HOW DOES IMAGERY WORK?

A single word describing a sense impression or a series of words describing complexes of sense impressions can rightly be considered when you are studying imagery. A single word naming a flower, say *rose*, evokes an image, because a person may visualize a rose and even recall its smell. He may also visualize a rose on a bush or in a bouquet, and associate the rose with love and respect which the rose may represent. More extensive imagery may stem from the description of a man running up a hill, because the reader may visualize the action, imaginatively hear the sound of the man's breathing, and even feel the fatigue of the person going up the hill.[1]

Imagery, in other words, is as complex as experience itself. An author tries to control imagery by presenting it in such a way that the reader will feel the right responses. For example, he may state that the man running up the hill is running to a telephone to report a serious highway accident. Then, when you imaginatively visualize the run, it may evoke feelings of intense, life-or-death urgency, and will probably not bring in any personal feelings you might have about running up a hill (Has the runner been trained properly to make the run? How does he pace himself? etc.). The author will control the context of the imagery in this way in order to evoke the proper emotion in you and to exclude any extraneous feelings you might attach to the image out of context. Indeed, a mark of a writer's skill is the way he controls the context of his imagery to achieve his effects, and you may evaluate him on his success or failure in this respect.

---

1 Images in the mind are also sometimes caused by abstract words that are commonly associated with concrete objects. For example, the word *friendship* might bring up the picture or memory of two close friends, or perhaps of one's own close friends. A legal word, such as *habeas corpus*, might similarly bring to mind the picture of a lawyer pleading before a judge that a prisoner be released. While it is not proper to regard abstract words like these as imagery, they do behave like imagery in many cases.

IMAGERY AND EXPOSITION

Imagery is important in both expository and imaginative writing. In fact, it would be difficult to find any good piece of writing that does not employ imagery to at least some extent. But imagery is most vital in imaginative writing, where it promotes immediate understanding and works importantly toward making suggestions and implications—non-logical processes that are not central to expository writing.

After the poet John Keats first read Chapman's translation of Homer, for example, he wrote a sonnet stating that he liked it. A fair expository restatement of his poem might be the following:

> I have read much European literature and have been told that Homer is the best writer of all, but, not knowing Greek, I couldn't appreciate his works until I read them in Chapman's translation. To me, this experience was an exciting discovery with extensive implications which I only dimly realized.

It is also fair to say that this paraphrase destroys Keats's poetry. Contrast the second sentence of the paraphrase with the last six lines of the sonnet as Keats wrote them:

> Then felt I like some watcher of the skies
> When a new planet swims into his ken;
> Or like stout Cortez when with eagle eyes
> He stared at the Pacific—and all his men
> Looked at each other with a wild surmise—
> Silent, upon a peak in Darien.

Notice that Keats did not say, as did the paraphrase, that he felt the excitement of a great discovery; instead he used imagery to show and to objectivize his feelings, so that the reader might re-experience feelings similar to his own. The prose paraphrase does not demonstrate the feelings sufficiently, but the use of imagery allows the reader to experience and visualize exciting moments of great discovery, and thereby to share the poet's attitudes. Most of us have difficulty in seeing things as others see them, and therefore we are often indifferent when someone tells us of his emotions. If Keats had said only "I felt excited," his poem would probably not cause anything but skepticism or boredom in us, because we would find no descriptions of objects from which we could reconstruct the precise degree of Keats's emotion. But we certainly can respond to the situation that Keats's imagery causes us to visualize. Imagery, in other words, conveys a close approximation of experience itself, and it calls forth the most strenuous imaginative responses from the reader. In fact, a person cannot regard himself as a good reader until he can re-experience what the writer shows through his imagery.

IMAGERY AND EFFECTIVENESS

Not only may imagery be embodied in single words or in descriptions —it is more notably found in figures of speech such as *simile* and *metaphor*. You are certainly acquainted with these terms, and know that the writer will use simile and metaphor to make his work more effective. By describing a situation analogous to the one at hand, he makes you more fully aware of the import of his situation, and can also cause certain desired emotional effects in you. In the six lines from Keats, for example, there are two similes, each embodying an extensive and illuminating image. In the following passage from Shakespeare's *Antony and Cleopatra,* you will see the effects of a rapidly moving series of images:

> The hearts
> That [spaniel'd] me at heels, to whom I gave
> Their wishes, do discandy, melt their sweets
> On blossoming Caesar; and this pine is bark'd,
> That overtopp'd them all.
> —IV, xii, 20–24

The word *hearts* in the first line is a *synecdoche* (a rhetorical figure whereby a small part is understood to mean also the large part). Whereas Antony's followers all had hearts, his mention of hearts also means the followers. The image implies (a) that his followers seemed to be fully committed to him ("with all their hearts"), and (b) that they stayed with him through emotion and not principle, and therefore they found it easy to leave him when their emotions had shifted.[2] The imagery evoked by the metaphor "discandy, melt their sweets" implies that these followers were sugary sweet toward him, but that now they have lost their form, are syrupy, and are literally flowing over the young Caesar, who is described by the metaphor "blossoming" as a flower just coming into bloom. The final image is from the experience of woodsmen. Antony has been tall and firm as a pine, but now his strength has been stripped from him, and he will inevitably die. In such ways images cause a completeness of statement and implication that literal language could approximate only with many more words, and then not as well.

Similes and metaphors may become complicated by *allusion* when a

---

2 The word *spaniel'd* in line 21 is a conjectural emendation by one of Shakespeare's editors, but it is a powerful comparison of dogs and Antony's followers that would be worthy of Shakespeare's imaginative genius, and it is very likely the word that Shakespeare used.

writer uses an image from another source in order to make his own context more effective, or to make it more learned. The original source, having been used in this way, then becomes a vital part of the writer's context. In Donne's sonnet "I Am a Little World Made Cunningly," for example, the concluding lines are:

> . . . burn me, O Lord, with a fiery zeal
> Of Thee and Thy house, which doth in eating heal.

The problem raised by the paradox in the last line is partially solved when you realize that the image in the metaphor is from Psalms 69, 9: "For the zeal of thine house hath eaten me up." Until the Biblical image is known, however, the line will be extremely difficult to visualize and understand completely.

This example brings up the problem of the amount of definition necessary for a full comprehension of imagery. For the most part your attempt to visualize, smell, taste, touch, and hear the experience described or suggested will suffice to convey the meaning of the imagery to you. In these cases a dictionary is superfluous. But an allusive image, like the Biblical one in Donne's poem, or an image which is archaic may require a dictionary in addition to any explanatory notes supplied by the editor of the work you are reading. As an example, let us look briefly at these lines from Pope's *Essay on Criticism:*

> Some, to whom Heav'n in Wit has been profuse,
> Want as much more, to turn it to its use;
> For *Wit* and *Judgment* often are at strife,
> Tho' meant each other's Aid, like *Man* and *Wife.*
> 'Tis more to *guide* than *spur* the Muse's Steed;
> Restrain his Fury, than provoke his Speed;
> The winged Courser, like a gen'rous Horse,
> Shows most true Mettle when you *check* his Course.
>
> —lines 80–87

Pope has sometimes been dispraised by the assertion that he was not an imaginative poet, but instead was ratiocinative or "discursive." A close look at a passage like this one renders this assertion absurd. Pope is talking about the relationship of reason to imagination, and is stating, briefly, that judgment (the perceptive, critical, discriminating faculty) must always be in control of imagination (or *fancy,* the other common word for the faculty, which is related to the words *fanciful* and *fantastic*). Pope compares judgment to a rider upon a race horse. All the strength and speed of a thoroughbred ("gen'rous Horse") are of no value, he says, unless a good jockey rides and paces it well. In line 86 Pope mentions "The winged Courser" (a flying horse) and opens the door to allusion. By re-

ferring to a classical dictionary, you can learn that the flying horse of
antiquity was Pegasus, who was ridden by Bellerophon in his fight against
the monster Chimaera. Bellerophon was assisted in his fight by the gods,
particularly by Athena, who was the goddess of wisdom. Other references
may also apply. A dictionary tells you that the word *chimerical* (fan-
tastically unreal) is derived from the name of the monster. The editor
may tell you that in the seventeenth and eighteenth centuries pure fantasy
was regarded as being akin to madness. In the context of the time when
Pope wrote, therefore, this allusion to the winged horse seems to be saying this: "If you wish to avoid madness or just foolishness in your writing, and if you wish to be favored by the goddess of wisdom, you must
guide your imagination by judgment." Thus Pope's imagery works in two
ways, literal and allusive, to strengthen his point that judgment is necessary in works of imagination and criticism.

You can see that reference books and annotated editions can be in-
dispensable in guiding you to an understanding of at least some of the
implications of an author's imagery. You may justifiably ask how you can
learn about allusions when you don't recognize them. The answer is to
read a good, annotated text and to look up all words and references that
are not immediately familiar to you. There are responsible, "definitive"
editions of most writers either available or in process of publication. See
the card catalogue in your library to find out about these editions.

YOUR THEME

Your job in preparing this theme, as always, is to be alert and to employ all facilities which can aid your understanding and appreciation.
You must study your poem or passage word by word. Savor each word and
set up a classification of what sorts of responses the words elicit. You
might set up a series of lists headed by the words *Sight, Smell, Taste,
Hearing, Touch,* and *Combinations* (how could you classify the image
"embalmed darkness" except by this latter category?). Then check yourself: Can you visualize a word or description? Can you recall a touch or
taste similar to that which the words describe? Try, for example, to visualize the word *beautiful,* or *beautiful day;* notice that both terms are abstract, and can mean many things, but that you can put them together
with other words to convey a fairly exact sense impression: *beautiful day
in winter at the ski resort.* As another example, try these lines:

> Veiled Melancholy has her sovran shrine,
>   Though seen of none save him whose strenuous tongue
> Can burst Joy's grape against his palate fine. . . .
>   —Keats, "Ode on Melancholy," lines 26–28

The first line is difficult to visualize, but the experience of bursting a grape against the palate draws your attention vividly to impressions of both taste and texture (i.e., touch).

With images that cause visual responses you might aid your imagination by drawing sketches. Some people might object to sketching images on the grounds that it tends to limit your responses too narrowly, but if it aids you in responding to a work, it is not despicable. The following line from Shakespeare's Sonnet 146, for example, offers an interesting challenge to the imagination that might be aided by a sketch:

> So shalt thou [the speaker's Soul] feed on
> Death that feeds on men, . . .
>   —line 13

Just how far does the image invite complete visualization? That is one problem faced by the student with a theme to write about this poem. Do the words *feed* and *feeds* invite a response visualizing an eater, while eating, being eaten, or should the words be read without the reader's attempting to imagine specific feeders? One student responded to these lines with the following drawing:

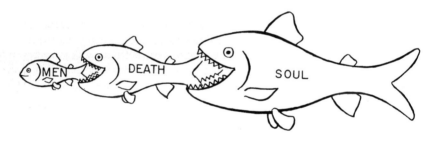

This drawing vividly shows the relationships involved, though it tends to demean Soul, Death, and Men (perhaps the student was thinking that men, in this case, are "poor fish"). Whether or not you carry your visualization this far, however, it is clear that Shakespeare's speaker is calling Death voracious because it seizes men for prey. But he is also asserting that the Soul can be equally voracious and more powerful than Death, even though it is also dependent upon Death for its sustenance.

Whether you make a drawing or use your ability to visualize the impressions suggested by the words, you are concerned in your analysis to see the effect of imagery in the work. How does the imagery convey meaning? What particular attitudes does it communicate or suggest? (That is, how do you feel about Death and the Soul after reading the line from Shakespeare? Or how do you feel about Keats's excitement presented in "On First Looking into Chapman's Homer"?) How fully developed are the images? Do they stem from single words, or are they developed at

greater length throughout a line or several lines, or perhaps even throughout the entire work? Are there many images, few images? Do the images
make the work particularly powerful, feeble? Why? Does the imagery at
one point in the poem create any special effect upon other parts of the
poem? Does the imagery seem to develop in any special pattern? (For example, Robert Frost's poem "Out, Out—" develops a pattern of sound
beginning with the noisy, snarling buzz saw and ending with the feeble
heartbeat of the dying boy; after the boy's death, Frost's description of
the people turning away contains no words describing sound; the poem
ends in silence, just as the boy's heart is now silent.) These are the questions that you should try to answer in your theme.

THE ORGANIZATION OF YOUR THEME

Introduction

In your introduction you ought to make a brief statement about the
nature of the work you are analyzing. Related to this will be your central
idea, which is the statement of the main point you wish to illustrate
about the imagery (i.e., that it is mainly visual, or that it makes the poem
powerful, or that it is ineffective, or some other point that your analysis
has uncovered).

Body

There are a number of approaches to discussing imagery, and you may
choose whatever method, or combination of methods you wish. Here are
some possible choices:

A. Discussion of all the kinds of responses caused by the imagery. Here you
should show the variety of imagery in the work, and draw a conclusion about
the type of imagery that predominates. Does the work appeal to all five senses?
Does one type (sight, hearing, etc.) predominate? What can you conclude from
your findings?
B. Discussion of the frames of reference of the imagery. Here you might show
the locations from which the images are derived. Does the writer favor images
from nature, from high society, from low society, from warfare, from politics,
from finance, from his reading, etc.? What conclusions can you draw?
C. Discussion of the effect of one image, or series of images, upon the other
images and ideas in the poem. Usually you would pick an image that occurs
early in the work, and ask if this image affects the ideas or mood (tone) of the
work. Thus, the first paragraph of Swift's *Battle of the Books* (a prose work)
contains uncomplimentary images pertaining to the behavior of hungry dogs;
in this way Swift conveys the impression that the whole battle between the "An-
cients" and "Moderns" has a physiological origin that is anything but flatter-
ing. In an analysis of this sort, you would try to show the importance of the
single image throughout the work.

D. Discussion of the way imagery causes suggestions and implications to appear in the work. Here you should show how far the imagery carries your imagination, and also you ought to show the limits of the imagery. Show how the imagery affects and adds to a bare paraphrase.

Conclusion

In your conclusion you should give your general impressions. You might state how the imagery deepened your experience of the work or your insight into the nature of literature itself. In a more thorough analysis you might compare the imagery in the work you have analyzed with the imagery appearing in works written by the author at earlier or later points in his career. Conclusions of this kind can show much about a writer's development.

HINTS

Instead of trying to discuss every image in the work, concentrate on typical, unusual, and particularly important images.

Be prepared to relate the imagery to conclusions the author apparently expected you to reach. Always emphasize the ways in which the imagery brings out conclusions and attitudes.

It is desirable and helpful to reproduce your poem or passage, double-spaced, and to number its lines from 1 to the end. Refer to these line numbers in your theme.

Sample Theme

A Study of the Imagery in Swift's
"Description of the Morning"

Now hardly here and there an Hackney-Coach	1
Appearing, show'd the Ruddy Morn's Approach.	2
Now *Betty* from her Master's Bed had flown,	3
And softly stole to discompose her own.	4
The Slipshod Prentice from his Master's Door,	5
Had par'd the Dirt, and Sprinkled round the Floor.	6
Now *Moll* had whirl'd her Mop with dext'rous Airs,	7
Prepar'd to Scrub the Entry and the Stairs.	8
The Youth with Broomy Stumps began to trace	9
The Kennel-Edge, where Wheels had worn the Place.	10
The Smallcoal-Man was heard with Cadence deep,	11
'Till drown'd in Shriller Notes of Chimney-Sweep,	12
Duns at his Lordship's Gate began to meet,	13
And Brickdust *Moll* had Scream'd through half the Street.	14

The Turnkey now his Flock returning sees,   15
Duly let out a-Nights to Steal for Fees.   16
The watchful Bailiffs take their silent Stands,   17
And School-Boys lag with Satchels in their Hands.[3]   18

Swift's "Description of the Morning" may aptly be called a series of little moving pictures, some with sound but most purely visual. Except for lines 3 and 4, the point of view is fairly distant from the scene Swift's speaker (who seems to be a realist if not a satirist) describes, so that only those sounds reach his ears that are quite loud—either the rattle and clack of an early morning hackney coach or the cries of street vendors. Structurally, the first eight lines are concerned with moving from inside the London houses to the outside, so that the early images depict interior and doorstep scenes, while the later ones depict and record what is seen and heard outdoors. Though the selection is not without humor, the dominant impression is that London life in the morning, as described here, is seedy and low, with the implication that this impression is also true of life generally, if only people would think about life without deluding themselves. The entire poem is framed by images that suggest that adult man has a nature that is furtive and stealthy, though the only vicious man is the venal "Turnkey," who has let his prisoners out at night so that they may steal and rob, in return for which they will give him a share of their "take." Within this frame, the sights and sounds of the poem, though uniformly vivacious, describe a world of very fallible beings.

The frame of human frailty sets the tone of the poem. First there is "Betty" (a typical name for a chambermaid) who has found it either pleasant or, more probably, remunerative or even politic, to sleep with her master. But she has a reputation to keep, so she runs from his bed when she hears the hackney coach (a horse-drawn taxi) and goes to rumple her own bed to persuade others that she has slept in it all night. Her action is performed "softly," and, we may also assume, stealthily. But more serious actions appear, for example, in line 17. Bailiffs were officers of the law empowered to arrest those charged with debt. So they must naturally take their "Stands" silently, and wait silently during the day to see if anyone on their lists appears on the street. Then, presumably, like tigers they will spring to action. Swift uses a comic, related image in line 13. The "Duns" meeting at his Lordship's gate are either tradesmen or their representatives who have come to present bills for their services to his Lordship. The picture here is that his Lordship is one of those genteel members of the aristocracy who consider it degrading to pay their tradesmen (i.e., tailors, wig-makers, et al.). The Lord, in other words, is a deadbeat; his wrong is actually as great as that of the debtors who are hunted by the bailiffs, but his rank and station prevent his creditors from swearing

---

3 Harold Williams, ed., The Poems of Jonathan Swift (London: Oxford University Press, 1937), I, 124–125.

out warrants. In short, Swift includes his Lordship, and much of the falseness he represents, among the low and depressing images in his poem. Stealth and silence characterize Betty and the Bailiffs, but, presumably, the "Duns" are crying out for payment at his Lordship's gate.

This uncomplimentary picture is made almost depressing in the visual images from lines 5 through 10. Here we see the "Slipshod Prentice" resisting the day. The dirt is so thick on his master's door (probably it had been splashed there the previous day by passing coaches) that it must be "par'd" away. To keep dust down in the workshop, the apprentice must sprinkle the floor, which was presumably of dirt, not of wood. One can imagine here the unpleasant, musty smell that the odor of wet earth must have given to the interior of the shop. Though cleanliness is desirable, the process of making entryways and stairs clean is unpleasant, and the picture of Moll does not give a cheerful impression as she sets about her morning chore. The most depressing image, however, is that of the "Youth with Broomy Stumps," who is apparently scavenging along the edge of the "Kennel" (a drainage ditch). He is looking for items of any value that might have fallen there, and has an old, worn-out broom to sift the dirt from the items. Since the ditch caught a good deal of refuse, the boy is also subject to some bad smells, certainly of decaying food and perhaps even of excrement. The general unpleasantness of the apprentice has thus turned into repulsiveness; although one feels a certain pity for the boy who is presumably forced by his poverty to scavenge. The worn wheel ruts (line 10) at this point seem to typify the unchangeable quality of the previous descriptions. The social structure has always made grooves as it moves; as it passes it splashes mud upon the doors of tradesmen, and in its ruts it leaves offal for the poor to sift. Certainly there is little hope, little cause for optimism, for any of those who are being described.

These general observations are reinforced by the street sounds that Swift next describes. From lines 11 through 14 appear references to a number of sounds that lend a background of shrillness. The first sound is heard from the "Smallcoal-Man" who is advertising his wares (charcoal carried in a long sack) in a deep bass voice. Here Swift may be referring to an actual person, Thomas Britton, who was a well-known smallcoal-man who gave concerts and collected books at the time. If this suggestion is right, our image (of sight at least) may be made concrete, since drawings of Thomas Britton have been preserved; two of them may be seen in the *Oxford Companion to Music*.[4] A contemporary source also helps us to get a notion of the cries of the chimney sweeps. Apparently Swift's sweep was indulging himself in shrill high notes on the morning we see and hear. Addison, in *Spectator* No. 251 (two years after Swift's poem was published) described the sweeps thus:

---

[4] Percy Scholes, ed., *The Oxford Companion to Music,* 9th ed. (London: Oxford University Press, 1960), facing p. 225.

The Chimney-sweeper is confined to no certain Pitch; he sometimes utters himself in the deepest Base [sic], and sometimes in the sharpest Treble; sometimes in the highest, and sometimes in the lowest Note of the Gamut.[5]

The words sung by the sweep and by "Brickdust *Moll*" (i.e., a woman who sold brick dust to be used for cleaning knives) were apparently unintelligible, or so says Addison. The street vendors have an "idle Accomplishment which they all of them aim at, of Crying so as not to be understood" so that "People know the Wares they deal in rather by their Tunes than by their Words" (*Spectator*, p. 245). The sounds to which Swift refers must therefore have been often unintelligible, cacophonous, but, to eighteenth-century ears, meaningful.

As I have shown, Swift's statement is conveyed entirely by means of images. Never once does he say "London in the morning is a busy, grim, unpleasant place, where foolish, wretched, and even dishonest people live." Instead, he makes his statement indirectly, as a result of the imagery he has selected. One might add that Swift's imagery does not indicate scorn for the scene, but rather it shows objective, detached observation. This observation is too accurate to have been written by a man who hated what he describes. Ending the poem is the line, "And School-Boys lag with Satchels in their Hands." The boys, like boys since the beginning of time, are in no hurry to get to school. Such an image evokes a smile; but in the sense that one's school days are the preparation for his adult life, the adult world portrayed here is hardly one to race toward eagerly. To some degree the word "lag" conveys an image that really summarizes the poem: the boys are reluctant, just as the apprentice is reluctant, to begin the day. But, once the day is begun, it picks up activity and noises, though nobody, if he looked closely, would be entirely happy about it. It is very difficult to preserve any illusions in the world Swift has created in this poem.

---

5 G. Gregory Smith, ed., *The Spectator* (London: Everyman's Library, 1958), II, 244.

10

The Theme About Point of View
in a Literary Work

*P*OINT OF VIEW has been defined as the personal pronoun from which a story or poem is narrated. That is, a story told by an *I* has a first-person point of view, whereas the constant recurrence of *he*'s, *she*'s, and *they*'s marks a third-person point of view. The third-person point of view is called *omniscient* when the speaker seems to know everything that goes on in the minds of his characters, and *limited* when he confines himself only to observation or to one character's mind. In short stories, poems, and novels, a writer is free to select any point of view he chooses. In drama, however, the point of view is, with rare exceptions (such as the traditional soliloquy), best regarded as third-person limited, because a dramatist presenting action and dialogue cannot show a character's mind except by what is spoken or acted.

Point of view has also been described as the way in which a writer *authenticates* his material. When we read something we want to be convinced of its probability or authenticity. Therefore we want first-hand testimony rather than hearsay; we want to believe that we are witnessing events rather than having them described to us. Writers in the twentieth century have particularly attempted to create fiction that is, in point of view, realistic; they wish to give us the impression that we are observers, not listeners. In earlier times, writers devoted themselves similarly to the problem of authenticating their material, although they did not do so in quite the way of Conrad or Hemingway. Whereas modern writers approach point of view as a problem in storytelling, earlier writers approached it as a problem in rhetoric, following the Aristotelian idea that the speaker should pay great attention to the character he projects as his own *ethical proof* (see Aristotle, *Rhetoric*, I, 2, 1356ᵃ).

POINT OF VIEW AND OPINIONS

You must realize at the outset that point of view should be carefully distinguished from opinions or beliefs, though in popular usage point of view and opinions are frequently confused. Point of view refers to the position from which things are seen; in its broad sense, *position* comprises everything, including opinions, that affects the speaker as an observer. Point of view conditions opinions. Suppose that a speaker is blind, or deaf; suppose that he is a child, or an old man; suppose that he has just been married, or that he has been disappointed in love. The opinions of these speakers about a painting, a piece of music, or love, would be necessarily limited by their conditions as observers of these matters. Remember, therefore, that opinions are only a function of point of view. You might say that studying opinions is to study *effects,* while studying point of view is to study *causes.*

POINT OF VIEW, CHARACTER ANALYSIS, AND TONE

There are places at which point of view overlaps with *character analysis* (see Chapter 6) and *tone* (see Chapter 11). Thus any consideration of point of view must necessarily treat those character traits of the speaker which influence what he says. Similarly, point of view has the same relationship to tone that it has to opinions: tone reveals the attitudes of the speaker toward his material and toward his audience, and these attitudes must inevitably be a product of the speaker's point of view. When you consider these similarities, however, you should realize that there are differences in emphasis: character study emphasizes everything connected with character; tone emphasizes the way language and structure are manipulated to convey attitudes; point of view emphasizes the total vantage point from which things are perceived.

THE PURPOSE OF A THEME ABOUT POINT OF VIEW

The object of this theme is to cause you to observe the effect of point of view in a story or poem, with the implication that point of view is similarly influential in all literature. The basic questions you should answer are these: How have the speaker's attitude, knowledge, and limitations contributed to forming the literary work as it actually is? Has the point of view succeeded in making the work seem true, or authentic, or probable? Writing this theme should help increase your perceptions as a disciplined reader and, as always, should make you aware that literary study is a study of the creative process, an attempt to understand the artistic mind, and a way of appreciating literature.

PREPARATION FOR YOUR THEME

As you read the work assigned, you will perceive the point of view operating in the way in which certain actions are described. What words are used? Let us consider an example. A man walks into a room in which a party is taking place. How shall this act be described? A neutral observer might say, "The man came in and joined the party." An enemy might say, "The man intruded upon the company and dampened the spirit of the guests." The sweetheart of the man might say, "Even the artificial flowers bloomed when he walked in the room." You will quickly see that the words used to describe even this simple action will depend upon the speaker's attitude, and that the speaker will frequently employ highly connotative words in order to arouse a desired emotional response in his readers. The study of point of view should show how these effects have operated within an entire work in order to make the work seem true and authentic.

Your problem in reading, therefore, is to observe carefully not only the story, incidents, ideas, and commentary, but also the language used to convey these various elements. You must test the quality of the various words to see if you are expected to respond in any particular way. Then, when you have made your observations, you must develop them: What characteristics does the speaker have? How are these characteristics brought out? How do these characteristics determine the material in the story or poem? What details are selected for inclusion? How are they arranged in the work? What is the emotion or emotions in which the action and ideas are described, and do the emotions remain constant or do they shift? (Of these last two questions, one is structural and the other is concerned with tone. In determining the answer to either, however, you should always emphasize relationships with point of view.) How might the emotions have been different if a different speaker were telling the story? What can you learn about the present speaker from the contrast? The answers to questions like these, together with your consideration of the connotations of the diction, will be the subject of the theme.

THE ORGANIZATION OF YOUR THEME

Specifically, you should have the following elements in your theme: (a) an analysis of the speaker and the situation to which he is responding, and (b) an analysis of the speaker's effect upon the literary work, whether upon the form of the narrative argument, the ideas, or the diction. Bear in mind that there is always interaction of the speaker and the situation to which he responds; just as the speaker influences events and ideas, there are ideas and events that influence him.

Introduction

Your introduction should describe the situation in the literary work. You might answer some or all of these questions in making your description. Who is the speaker? What is the character and background of the speaker? What is his relationship to the material he is presenting? What is his relationship to the person listening to him (if there is a listener)? Does he speak directly to the reader or does he speak in such a way that you become either a witness or an eavesdropper? How much knowledge does the speaker take upon himself (i.e., does he write with the assumption that he knows what is going on in other people's minds, or does he confine himself to recording what he has heard, seen, smelled, tasted, felt)? Does the speaker ever rely on the information of others for his material? How reliable are these other witnesses? Is the speaker a participant in the action? Is he affected by the action? Is he the same at the end as he was at the beginning?

As you answer these questions you will arrive at a central idea about the speaker and his relationship to the material. The sample theme builds to the idea that the speaker's attitudes change as the circumstances in the poem change. Similarly, you might be writing on a story which describes the effects of mass hypnosis, and you may discover that the speaker himself has been hypnotized. Whatever you discover in this way should be the point that you develop in the remainder of your theme.

Body

In the body you should analyze the effect of the speaker on the situation and vice versa. Does the material proceed naturally or logically from the situation you describe in the introduction? How does the situation cause the speaker to respond? What evidence do you find of the speaker's emotional state? Is he emotionally involved in the situation or indifferent to it? Does he seem able or unable to judge it? What emotions are produced by the incidents, ideas, and language? Do you think that these emotions are appropriate to the speaker and to his reactions to the general situation in the work?

Conclusion

In your conclusion you should evaluate the success of the author's point of view: Was it consistent, effective, truthful? What did the writer gain (if anything) by his selection of point of view? What did he lose (if anything)? How might a less skillful writer have handled similar material? After answering questions like these, you may end your theme.

PROBLEMS IN WRITING YOUR THEME

1. In considering point of view, you will encounter the problem of whether to discuss the author or his speaker as the originator of the atti-

tudes. It is probably best always to discuss the speaker, with the proviso, of course, that the author is always manipulating the speaker, even if the speaker is in truth a phase of the author's personality. An author and his speaker are not necessarily the same; the *persona* is just as much a creation as the literary work itself. Witness, for example, the cases of Swift and Gulliver, Marlow and Conrad. There will naturally be many ideas common to both the author and his speaker, but your statements about these must be inferential, not absolute.

2. You may have a tendency to wander away from point of view into a summary or discussion of ideas. Emphasize the presentation of the events and ideas and the causes for this presentation. Do not emphasize the subject material itself, but use it only as it bears upon your consideration of point of view. Your object is not just to interpret the work, but also to show how the point of view enables you to interpret the work.

Inevitably you must talk about the material in the work, but use it only to illustrate your assertions about point of view. You should avoid the following pattern of statement, which will always lead you astray: "The speaker says this, which means this." You must instead adhere to this pattern, which will keep your emphasis always upon your central idea: "The speaker says this, which shows this about him and his attitudes." If a particular idea is difficult, you might need to explain it, but do not do so unless it illustrates your central idea.

Sample Theme

A Study of the Point of View
in Donne's Poem "A Feaver"

In this seven-stanza poem the speaker is talking directly to a woman —his beloved—who is seriously ill, in the grips of a fever that becomes progressively worse as he speaks. The reader is therefore made witness to an intensely dramatic situation, since the issues in the poem are first, life and death, and second, the relationship of the speaker to his beloved. What might be expected from human beings under the circumstances of the poem? A bit of cheer? Some flowers? Some statements evading the central fact of death? A reaffirmation of love? The speaker's loss of emotional control? Depending upon the seriousness of the illness, we might expect any or all of these from an ordinary person. But the speaker in this poem is not ordinary.

He reveals himself as an enlightened, educated, witty man, well grounded in Christianity, whose love is both profound and lifelong. When he speaks he preserves this character, and uses the language of his intellectuality to declare his love. He is losing his beloved, and his mood, at first reassuring and confident, accordingly sinks as this fact is

impressed upon him. But his final words are of love. The poem therefore records realistically the emotional shift of the speaker in response
to this dramatically moving situation, as I shall try to demonstrate.

In the opening stanza the speaker bravely faces the fact that his beloved might die, but his attitude is that she should not and will not.
He is, in short, trying to reassure his beloved, as anyone might do who
is visiting and comforting a sick person:

> Oh doe not die, for I shall hate
> All women so, when thou art gone,
> That thee I shall not celebrate,
> When I remember, thou wast one.[1]

Strong personalities these, that can joke this way in the face of death.
After this initial jocularity, the speaker for the next two stanzas creates
a complex and paradoxical mood of cheer, building upon the initial
directive that the beloved one should not die. Briefly, the speaker
demonstrates his intellectuality by creating a logical argument which
claims that the beloved not only should not, but cannot die, since the
definition of death ("To leave this world behind, is death.") does not
apply to her, for she *is* the world and cannot therefore leave herself
behind. Or, if she dies, then the remaining world—the earth we live on
—will be nothing but a "carkasse" and "corrupt wormes" since the beloved will be gone. Certainly, the relationship of the speaker and the
beloved must be an intellectual one. His estimation of her intelligence
is high, at any rate, for he expects her to follow the argument, which is
really the logical extreme of the lover's ordinary claim to his sweetheart, "You are all the world to me." Invalid as it is logically, this argument serves a higher kind of truth, since it establishes the closeness of
the emotional ties between the speaker and his beloved in a mood of
intellect against the backdrop of death.

At this point we may assume that the beloved one has been seized
with a painful attack, for the speaker during the next two stanzas
ceases to address her and instead makes an outcry to the "wrangling
schooles" that have been asking the cataclysmic question about the
fire that "Shall burne this world" (this is the question about the final
destruction of the universe). This question demonstrates the speaker's
complex mind, for he is able to apply it to the problem of an individual death. His mind, with its powers of analogy, is like lightning.
First he pursues the image of stanzas two and three, to ask whether his
beloved's fever might be the fire that will destroy the world. Then he
moves in this frame of reference into a cosmic compliment to her. His
logic is as follows: since his beloved is the world, and since she is being
consumed by the fire or fever, she will not "long beare this torturing

---

1 *The Complete Poetry and Selected Prose of John Donne & The Complete Poetry
of William Blake*, with an introduction by Robert Silliman Hillyer (New York: Random
House, Inc., 1946), p. 13. All quotations are taken from this page.

wrong," because fire needs much "corruption" as "fuell" upon which
to feed, and she is pure, and not corrupt (the speaker does not know
the theory of oxidation, since the poem was written early in the seventeenth century). Therefore, concludes the speaker, she cannot sustain
the fever, and will not suffer long because of it. Here, as he compliments her, the speaker is comforting himself—naturally, I think—since
no one wants to see a beloved one suffer, even if death is the only
release from pain. But the realization that death is near makes final
words necessary in the next stanzas. The speaker is shown to be a person who can say the proper words.

Since death is near, the time for speech is short, and the speaker is
forced to say everything to his beloved in two stanzas. He desires to
comfort and to compliment her, and claims that her "burning fits" are
like "meteors" that will burn out quickly, leaving her "unchangeable
firmament." Here his erudition and background are again apparent,
for he selects a Biblical word, *firmament*, which is rich with the connotations of the Creation, to show that his love is everlasting. We
notice that his description of his beloved has moved from the "world"
to the "firmament" as the entire poem moves toward death and the
(hopefully) heavenly reunion, which is never specifically mentioned.
We can see, however, that the speaker's attitudes toward death are contained within the limits of Christian orthodoxy.

In the concluding stanza the speaker asserts the power of his dream
of love. Though his hold upon the dying beloved one is tenuous, he
says, he desperately clings to it:

> Yet 't was of my minde, seising thee,
>   Though it in thee cannot persever.
> For I had rather owner bee
>   Of thee one houre, than all else ever.

He knew that he could not possess her forever, in other words, but he
dreamed that he could, because of his love for her. His deep despair
and helplessness finish the logic, and his final word is "ever," suggesting the eternity in which the beloved one, and eventually the speaker,
shall rest.

The poem, then, treats a difficult subject—the ultimate subject—
delicately and truthfully, from a consistent point of view. The poem
demonstrates how the human soul can react against the inevitable fact
of death, which most of us avoid, and before which most of us are
mute. The speaker's mind is therefore the real subject of the poem,
and through his mind runs the continuous image of his beloved as first
the world and finally the firmament. In lighter, happier moments, I
believe, this image could furnish extravagant praise and elaborate
compliments (as it does in other poems by Donne), but with the im-
mediacy of death it defines, finally, the value of love in life. Within
the subtle mind of the speaker—the point of view—the semiplayful

logic reveals truthfully the state of the person in love: namely the willingness to assert that deep love, possessed for just one hour, has more value than anything else the universe provides. The idea is not in the speaker's immediate thoughts at the start of the poem, but is verbalized only as the situation demands it. For this reason the poem portrays an intensely dramatic and genuinely true development of a vigorous, educated mind responding to sorrow and death.

11

The Theme Analyzing Tone

*T*ONE is one of the most important concepts to understand and describe in the study of literature. Ideally, tone refers to the means by which a writer conveys attitudes. Though it is a technical subject, in practice the discussion of tone becomes focused upon the attitudes themselves. For this reason, the terms *tone* and *attitude* are sometimes used synonymously. You should remember, however, that tone refers not to attitudes, but to that quality of a writer's style which reveals—or creates—these attitudes. If you preserve this distinction you should be able to handle a theme about tone and should quickly appreciate all its implications for literary study.

Studying and describing tone requires the greatest alertness and subtlety, because your understanding of tone will be dependent largely upon your ability to make inferences from the work you are reading (sometimes this process is called "reading between the lines"). Your analysis of tone is, in effect, your analysis of the author's mind at work, and through this analysis you can become aware of the vitality of literature—the profound, moving life of the author's mind as seen in his words. Reading a work of literature without perceiving its tone is like watching a speaker on television with the sound turned off; without tone you can guess at meaning, but cannot understand it fully.

TONE IN OPERATION

Tone in literature has been borrowed from the phrase *tone of voice* in speech. You have certainly heard this phrase, and may even have been criticized at one time or another for having said something in a certain tone of voice or for having indicated an attitude that has displeased a parent, friend, customer, or teacher. Tone of voice, in other words, is a reflection of your attitude toward the person or persons whom you are addressing and also toward the subject matter of your discussion. In the personal circumstances of speech, tone of voice is made up of many elements: the speed with which you utter your words, the enthusiasm—or lack of it—that you project into what you say, the pitch and loudness of your speech, your facial expressions, the way you hold your body, and your distance from the person to whom you are speaking.

Your attitudes are always basic to your opinions, friendships, activities, and even your deepest personal philosophy. Think briefly about the tone of these statements, which you may have heard or said: "Don't call me; I'll call you." "Oh, yes, I would be absolutely overjoyed to make the beds, do this morning's dishes, and sweep and mop the floor." Or imagine that before an examination a good friend tells you, "I hope you get the grade you deserve on the test." You may wonder about his exact meaning. To make it clear, he may accompany his words with a roguish smile which makes you see that your friendship is not without a certain degree of antagonism. He wishes you to do well, yet he would probably not grieve uncontrollably if you did not. But perhaps you realize that your friendship is sound if he feels safe in expressing his complexity of attitudes toward you. All these situations, and many more that you could supply yourself, require a consideration of tone.

As a literary comparison, let us look briefly at this passage from *Gulliver's Travels,* written by one of the great masters of tone in English literature:

> Imagine with thy self, courteous Reader, how often I then wished for the Tongue of *Demosthenes* or *Cicero,* that might have enabled me to celebrate the Praise of my own dear native Country in a Style equal to its Merits and Felicity.[1]

You have here a passage in which Gulliver is perfectly sincere about praising England, whereas Swift the satirist, behind the scenes, is just about to deliver a satiric condemnation of the England of his day. The control of tone makes these contrasting attitudes evident, and makes this passage comic. Swift controls the tone by causing Gulliver to refer to the two most famous ancient orators who, beyond their ability to speak well, were also known for their powers to condemn. He also makes Gulliver use the ambiguous phrase "equal to its Merits and Felicity" and the possibly sarcastic word "celebrate." The tone here is quite similar to that in the previously mentioned banter with the imaginary friend, with this difference: in the literary work you are not aided by the physical, conversational context of the interchange. All you have is the printed page; to interpret it properly you have only a dictionary, other reference works, and, above all, your intelligence.

Tone, of course, may be described in many ways, as there are many human moods. Here is a partial list of words that might describe tone in particular passages:

---

1 Robert A. Greenberg, ed., *Gulliver's Travels: An Annotated Text With Critical Essays* (New York: W. W. Norton & Co., Inc., 1961), II, vi , 103.

simple, straightforward, direct, unambiguous
complicated, complex, difficult
forceful, powerful
ironic, sardonic, sarcastic
indirect, understated, evasive
bitter, grim
sympathetic, interested
indifferent, unconcerned, apathetic
antagonistic, hostile
violent, outraged, indignant, angry
elevated, grand, lofty
serious, solemn, sepulchral, ghoulish
comic, jovial, easy, friendly.

A thesaurus would supply you with many more words, and it is conceivable that there are, somewhere, literary works to which all the words you discover might be applied.

PROBLEMS IN DESCRIBING TONE

The study of tone is the study of the ways in which attitudes are manifested in a particular literary work. Therefore, when you write a theme about tone, you must attempt to name and describe these attitudes and analyze the means by which they are expressed. Your statements will be based upon inferences that you make from the text.

You must also attempt to describe the intensity, the force with which the attitudes are expressed. This task is difficult, but necessary, and it is one of the ways by which you can amplify your statements about the nature of the attitudes. The force of the tone depends upon the intrinsic seriousness of the situation, the speaker's degree of involvement in it, and his control over his expression. You would recognize the differences in intensity between the following columns:

1	2
"This report is not what we expected."	"This report is terrible."
"Mr. Student, your paper shows promise, but it is not, as yet, up to passing standards."	"Mr. Student, your paper is a slovenly disgrace."

In describing the difference, you would necessarily concentrate on the differing *intensities* of the tones expressed in the quotations. Or, compare the intensities of tone implicit in these two quotations:

1. Spoken in Cuba: "Yankee, go home."
2. Spoken in Paris: "Yankee, go home—via Air France."

These last quotations bring up another, closely related, element in the consideration of tone—namely, that of control. A writer may feel deeply about a subject, but if he completely gives vent to his feelings he is likely to create not a literary work but only an emotional display. He must always control the expression of sentiment, because his appeal must be not only to his readers' sympathies but also to their understanding. A fine example of the control of attitude is *Antony and Cleopatra* (V, ii). Cleopatra is about to commit suicide. Just before she does, Shakespeare introduces a rustic on stage to bring her the asp. The resulting interchange between Cleopatra, serious and about to die, and the stupid but concerned clown is clearly designed to arouse laughter. The problem in interpreting this scene is that of Shakespeare's attitude toward Cleopatra and toward his audience. It is likely that Shakespeare introduced the comic scene in order to keep his treatment of Cleopatra from becoming purely sentimental. He knew that one way to produce laughter is to heap misfortune upon misfortune, so that an audience will ultimately respond to additional misfortunes with laughter, not with sympathy. Cleopatra's suicide is the final misfortune, and, lest his audience not respond with sorrow, Shakespeare provides the clown to siphon off, as it were, his audience's tension by giving it a legitimate release in laughter. In this way he directs a proper amount of sympathy toward Cleopatra and deepens our concern for her. The situation is complex, but Shakespeare's handling of it indicates the control of the master.

For the greatest skill of the writer is often his courage to treat a serious problem in a light or comic way. By doing so he maintains proportion, shows control, and makes his work generally effective. Shakespeare must have had great confidence in his own ability to evaluate dramatic situations to succeed with this comic scene. You may remember similar situations in your own life. Have you ever had the impulse to insult a friend, parent, or a "steady" date? In friendly banter, however, you always assume that your friend will be able to see through your "insult" into your genuine fondness. Treatment like this is usually called *irony*. In literature, as in friendship, irony implies a compliment by the writer to the reader, for it indicates that the writer assumes skill and intelligence on his reader's part sufficient to see through the surface statement into the seriousness beneath. Irony implies that the writer has great control over his material and much confidence in his readers. Sir Winston Churchill, for example, has been quoted as saying, "Democracy is the worst type of government, except all the rest." His ironic statement implies great understanding of human imperfections; it implies that man is in a process of evolving and endeavoring to perfect his political institutions; but it also implies respect for democracy and for those who love it. The statement shows great control over tone.

IDENTIFYING TONE IN LITERATURE

As you have undoubtedly concluded, the study of tone is quite general. It requires a study of everything in a literary work that might contribute more than just the denotative statement. To perceive tone, therefore, you must be completely alert. You must be constantly aware of the general impression that a passage leaves with you, but you must also be analytical enough to study the particular ways by which this effect is achieved. You must understand all the words; you must read the work carefully, then study the passages you select for discussion in order to determine the connotations of the words and the rhythms of the cadence groups. Anything might present an illustration of tone, and to understand the tone you must respond to everything.

Look at this passage from Lytton Strachey's biography of Florence Nightingale in *Eminent Victorians*,[2] a work known for its tone:

> Eventually the whole business of purveying to the hospitals was, in effect, carried out by Miss Nightingale. She alone, it seemed, whatever the contingency, knew where to lay her hands on what was wanted; she alone could dispense her stores with readiness; above all, she alone possessed the art of circumventing the pernicious influences of official etiquette. This was her greatest enemy, and sometimes even she was baffled by it. On one occasion 27,000 shirts, sent out at her instance by the Home Government, arrived, were landed, and were only waiting to be unpacked. But the official "Purveyor" intervened; "he could not unpack them," he said, "without a Board." Miss Nightingale pleaded in vain; the sick and wounded lay half-naked, shivering for want of clothing; and three weeks elapsed before the Board released the shirts. A little later, however, on a similar occasion, Miss Nightingale felt that she could assert her own authority. She ordered a Government consignment to be forcibly opened, while the "Purveyor" stood by, wringing his hands in departmental agony.

The tone here conveys admiration and respect for Miss Nightingale, as contrasted with the attitude of contempt for the official incompetence against which she had to work. Notice the diction Lytton Strachey employs in conveying his attitude toward her: "she alone," "readiness," "even she," "pleaded," "felt that she could assert," "ordered." These words are to be contrasted with those used in description of the officialdom: "pernicious influences," "baffled," official 'Purveyor'," "three weeks elapsed before the Board released the shirts," "wringing his hands in departmental agony." When these opposite series of words are placed in the context of "the sick and wounded lay half-naked, shivering for want of clothing," their opposition is made even more apparent. Lytton Strachey does not

---

2 (New York: Harcourt, Brace & World, Inc., 1918), pp. 146–147.

say directly that Florence Nightingale was heroic, yet his *tone* clearly indicates that he thought she was. Diction is the principal way by which he has communicated his tone, which is clear and unambiguous.

Take another instance, this time from the Old English poem "The Wanderer," in a modern prose translation by Professor R. K. Gordon: [3]

> Whither has gone the horse? Whither has gone the man? Whither has gone the giver of treasure? Whither has gone the place of feasting? Where are the joys of hall? Alas, the bright cup! Alas, the warrior in his corslet! Alas, the glory of the prince! How that time has passed away, has grown dark under the shadow of night, as if it had never been! Now in the place of the dear warriors stands a wall, wondrous high, covered with serpent shapes; the might of the ash-wood spears has carried off the earls, the weapon greedy for slaughter—a glorious fate; and storms beat upon these rocky slopes; the falling storm binds the earth, the terror of winter. Then comes darkness, the night shadow casts gloom, sends from the north fierce hailstorms to the terror of men. Everything is full of hardship in the kingdom of earth; the decree of fate changes the world under the heavens. Here possessions are transient, here friends are transient, here man is transient, here woman is transient; all this firm-set earth becomes empty.

The imagery here indicates the tone—one of despair for the prosperity of man in his earthly state. Complementing the imagery is a series of abstractions which indicate the effect of the hailstorms and darkness upon the minds of men. This semantic interpretation is augmented by the rhythms of the original (faithfully preserved in the translation). The statements are short, even abrupt at the end. The impression is given that the earth definitely holds terror for mankind. There are no subordinate clauses in which the poet might express any qualifications or exceptions to the examples he has given. Thus, the diction, sentence structure, and rhythm contribute to the tone of despair.

Unlike the passage from *Gulliver's Travels,* which is ironic and ambiguous, the tone in these last two examples is straightforward and positive.

Our analysis of these examples was largely concerned with style, but tone may also be caused by the sheer weight of accumulated evidence. The multiplication of examples in support of a claim effects a tone of certainty, and the constant insistence upon some attitude produces a tone of solid conviction. As an example, look at the sermon on hell by Father Arnall in Chapter III of Joyce's *Portrait of the Artist as a Young Man,* where the tone is firm, solid, and inescapable. Few persons can read this section without being emotionally shaken by the sheer weight of the evidence presented by Father Arnall. Or think briefly about Thoreau's assertions throughout *Walden* that our industrial civilization is lifeless and artificial.

---

3 *Anglo-Saxon Poetry,* Rev. ed., Everyman's Library No. 794 (New York: E. P. Dutton & Co., Inc., 1954), pp. 74–75.

Upon reading this book, one is swayed by the tone either to assent to Thoreau's position or else to question his own position thoroughly. It is difficult to imagine that a reader could be unaffected in any way by Thoreau's tone.

It is fair to conclude that tone is an integral part of meaning and literary excellence. Tone controls responses, and your responses are essential in your literary experience. Control over tone distinguishes plain statement from artistic statement. As you analyze the tone of a work you will realize that the degree of a writer's control over tone provides a strong basis for evaluating his stature as a writer.

YOUR APPROACH TO TONE

Your main problem in reading the work assigned is to determine to your satisfaction what the dominant tone is. You must therefore carefully examine not only what is said, but the context in which it is said. In order to support your claim about tone, you will need to study those factors (style, structure, idea) which cause the particular tone that you have noted.

The amount of analysis you do will depend upon the length of the work you are discussing. In a long work you might analyze representative passages which support your central idea. If the work is short, perhaps a short poem, you might very well attempt to analyze the entire work.

Once you have determined your interpretation of the tone, you should state that as your central idea. Then, without making distortions, you should gather material which will support your central idea. Let the material produce the idea. Do not neglect material that opposes your idea. So long as what you analyze has bearing upon your central idea, you might bring in considerations of style, ambiguity, accumulation of evidence—all at one time. Just remember to point your discussion toward your basic argument.

Beyond the single statement (your central idea) about tone, you might very well discover that the tone in your literary work is made up of a complexity of moods, a progression of tones. An excellent critical article has been written describing a progression of tone in the poetry of Pope,[4] and an entire book has been written to show that a typical poem by John Donne is structurally dependent upon a complex progression of attitudes.[5] In your theme, if your central idea is that there is a complexity of tone or progression of attitudes, you would simply construct your argument to demonstrate the validity of your claim.

---

[4] Maynard Mack, "The Muse of Satire," *Yale Review* (1951), XLI, 80–92.

[5] Leonard Unger, *Donne's Poetry and Modern Criticism* (Chicago: Henry Regnery Co., 1950).

THE ORGANIZATION OF YOUR THEME

The main problem in your discussion of tone is that your remarks are based upon inferences. You cannot, therefore, state absolutely that your author actually *held* a certain attitude; you can instead only *infer* that he held that attitude. Your theme is not biographical, but interpretive. Be aware that your inferences might result as much from your own attitudes as from those of the author. For example, recent attempts to interpret the tone in Chaucer's *Prioress's Tale* have implied that, because Chaucer treats the Prioress with gentle irony in the *General Prologue,* he was hostile to the anti-Jewish sentiment expressed in her story. It would seem that, in their attempt to make Chaucer as tolerant of the Jewish faith as a modern intelligent person should be, many readers have read their own enlightenment into Chaucer's work. But if you remember that great writers generally held views that were current at their times, and that their attitudes may not coincide exactly with your own, you will be properly cautious in making remarks about tone.

One further caution: keep your central idea uppermost in your reader's mind. You must inevitably talk about what has happened in the work you have read, but bring in these references *only* to illustrate and amplify your remarks about tone. Never forget your point; never descend to mere summary.

Introduction

State your central idea. You should not only define the tone briefly, but also describe the force and conviction of the tone. Your thesis sentence should be a statement about the areas into which you plan to develop your discussion. If there are any particular obstacles to the proper determination of the tone, either in the work or in your personal attitudes, you ought to state these in your introduction also.

Body

This should be a pointed discussion of the major elements in the work that caused you to arrive at your central idea. You are free to organize this section in any way you wish. Two suggested methods are: *A.* If there is a unity of tone throughout the work, you ought to organize the body in order to show the scope of the tone; that is, you would use various sections of the work as a basis for showing how widely the tone permeates the work. Or you might wish to illustrate the depth of the attitudes. In this plan, you would analyze a few passages (be sure that they are representative) in order to show how deeply and with how much conviction the attitudes are manifested in the work. *B.* If there is a shift of tone, or if there is a complexity of tone within the work, you might organize the body of your theme in order to mirror the shift or complexity. The sample theme asserts that there is a complexity of attitudes in the work it analyzes. This theme is organized to show how the meaning is made clear despite this complexity. The tone in good writing is often complex.

Conclusion

The principal object of your conclusion is to relate the question of tone to your understanding and evaluation of the work. Elements to consider in evaluation are (a) the intensity and (b) the control over attitudes.

Sample Theme

An Analysis of the Tone in Section IX of Swift's *Tale of a Tub*

The tone in the "Digression concerning the Original, the Use and Improvement of *Madness* in a Commonwealth"—Section IX of *A Tale of a Tub*—is steadily and grimly ironic. The tone results from Swift's *persona*'s being a madman who advocates mad views. Combining this fact with the logical inference that Swift's values are to be found in the reversal of whatever the madman says, the reader can perceive Swift's relentless irony. This irony is intensely bitter, mixed with hysterical, violent, repulsive, and sometimes indecent humor. Yet surprisingly, there is an overall note of encouragement, which results from the reverse side of this same irony.

The irony can be seen through the speaker's main idea: a madman himself, he has conceived a plan that grows logically out of his previous treatment of Jack, the "reformed" brother ("A Person whose Intellectuals were overturned, and his Brain shaken out of its Natural Position" [6]). His pet theory is that madness has produced everything and everyone that the world has ever considered "great" and "noble"; that is, military conquests, schemes of science and philosophy, great statesmen, courtiers, warriors, and men of high fashion. Since madness has caused such greatness, he says, let us have a committee to examine the madmen in Bedlam (the London house for the insane) and put them to use where they can employ their madness to the highest ends, just as society has always used madmen. That is the scheme in brief, and one can easily perceive Swift's tone, which mocks conventional definitions of "greatness." The tone shows that Swift's values are to be found in praise of sanity, in praise of eliminating madness in high places, and

---

[6] A. C. Guthkelch and David Nichol Smith, eds., *A Tale of a Tub*, 2nd ed. (London: 1958), p. 162. All page numbers refer to this edition.

in praise of making people accept balanced, sane men as their political and philosophical leaders. Though this statement gives an idea of Swift's values and attitudes, however, it falls far short of describing the power, the force, with which Swift communicates his ideas.

Mockery of human society—its popular illusions, its scientific methods, its ways of carrying out recommendations, its ways of insuring domestic tranquillity and promoting the general welfare—is the dominant mood of Swift's satire. The mockery is evident, for example, in the pseudoscientific form of the "Digression" itself. Like a committee report, the plan of the "Digression" is logical; it moves from a preposterous hypothesis, quietly understated, into supporting evidence, followed by a plan for action together with specific recommendations for carrying it out. But the reader's perception of the mockery is complicated by his gnawing feeling that the preposterous is true. For the irony appears through the logic of the argument: though the hypothesis seems at first to be mad, the sequence of supporting examples is entirely logical. Is logic therefore mad? But we believe in logic. Or is the hypothesis mad? We would like to think so, but what other than madness, one might ask with the mad speaker, could cause a great king to want to "take and lose Towns; beat Armies, and be beaten: drive Princes out of their Dominions; fright Children from their Bread and Butter; burn, lay waste, plunder, dragoon, massacre Subject and Stranger, Friend and Foe, Male and Female" (p. 165)? Yet this king, Louis XIV, is acknowledged in the world's eyes to be great; and war as an instrument of foreign policy is still accepted by all nations.

The tone thus makes the reader squirm in embarrassed amazement. In the "recommendations" part of the "Digression" the tone makes him squirm again. There the speaker advances his propositions for putting madmen to use. Since he is perfectly sincere, quiet, and deferential, he arouses belief, while Swift's condemnation becomes more exact and therefore more cutting and barbed. In these quiet, pseudoreasonable words, there lurks the violent lash of the master satirist, flaying the exposed carcass of the beaulike society, and showing the vapidity and madness beneath the skin.

For the tone ultimately brings relentless self-awareness. Swift's madman has hit upon exactly what is wrong in the world as it is, and Swift's irony is that this madman supports it; in fact, he wishes to keep the world mad and to make it more so. But if the madman's world is our world, which we support, then what is the state of our sanity? As this madman makes his preposterous analysis, and advances his insane scheme for the "betterment" of society, Swift makes the reader understand the root causes of mankind's ills. In the speaker's erratic but scholarly way, interspersed freely with low images that reduce all illusions to the manure pile, the speaker assumes that because things are as they are, they are right, while the reader comes increasingly to object at the moment of assenting to what this former inmate of Bedlam says. This tension produces one of the most grimly comic moods in the "Digression." Seizing the idea that "great men" are made by a lucky confluence of their madness with the opportunity to use it in a socially approved way, Swift's speaker brings out one of the fundamental points in his mad argument, but, says the irony, is he not right?

> . . . there is a peculiar *String* in the Harmony of Human Understanding, which in several individuals is exactly of the same Tuning. This, if you can dexterously screw up to its right Key, and then strike gently upon it; Whenever you have the Good Fortune to light among those of the same Pitch, they will by a secret necessary Sympathy, strike exactly at the same time. And in this one Circumstance, lies all the Skill or Luck of the Matter; for if you chance to jar the String among those who are either above or below your own Height, instead of subscribing to your Doctrine, they will tie you fast, call you Mad, and feed you with Bread and Water.
>
> —pp. 167–168

The irony leads virtually to grim despair in that anti-Apollonian part of the "Digression" where the speaker advances logical reasons for preserving a superficial view of life and its problems, and avoiding a deep analysis of them. His logic, well buttressed by supporting examples, again creates the tone, which becomes a combination of both the affirmative and the negative. Since looking inside things makes people see only their ugliness, he says, it is necessary to avoid all looking into things. Let people see the surface only, and then they will be happy, as most people define happiness. Let them gloss over truth; let them imagine themselves better than they are or ever can be; let them never know themselves:

> . . . He that can with *Epicurus* content his Ideas with the *Films* and *Images* that fly off upon his Senses from the *Superficicies* of Things; Such a Man truly wise, creams off Nature, leaving the Sower and the Dregs, for Philosophy and Reason to lap up. This is the sublime and refined Point of Felicity, called, *the Possession of being well deceived;* The Serene Peaceful State of being a Fool among Knaves.
>
> —p. 174

Here there is an incredible control of the violence of feeling. After all, Swift's speaker is degrading the things that Swift himself must hold most dear (the speaker equates Reason and Philosophy with dogs or cats lapping up dregs), while the speaker concludes that self-delusion is a normal condition. Swift's indignation is restrained; his scalpel is sharp; his incision is clean; but will the patient, society, be cured?

Just as the heavy irony approaches despair over the patient's prospects, it also points the way to a cure. For if the reversal of madness is sanity, the reversal of despair is joy. There is a way to make society recuperate, and it is not the one put forth by the speaker. Swift suggests the method by the reversal of values implicit in the ironic tone. Shining through is the appeal to sanity, the appeal to know oneself.

The mood of the "Digression" brightens, therefore, because of this passage at mid-point:

> . . . For, the Brain, in its natural Position and State of Serenity, disposeth its Owner to pass his Life in the common Forms, without any Thought of subduing Multitudes to his own *Power,* his *Reasons,* or his *Visions;* and the more he shapes his Understanding by the Pattern of Human Learning, the less he is inclined to form Parties after his particular Notions; because that instructs him in his private Infirmities, as well as in the stubborn Ignorance of the People.
>
> —p. 171

There can be optimism, implies Swift himself now, speaking through the tone. If only men will follow the "Pattern of Human Learning" and look into things, ugly as they sometimes are, they will see the truth. If only men will not delude themselves, particularly into seeking power over others, or be deceived by those who are themselves deluded, they can find truth and that middle way that will save them. For truth and moderation give the only foundation for society; anything less is madness.

The tone of despair thus, everywhere, gives way to hope, but a qualified hope, since the speaker's statement that Reason is "a very light Rider, and easily shook off" (p. 180) is undeniably right in the context of the "Digression" and of the general history of the world analyzed there. Though the melioristic mood is thus only anticipatory and incomplete, no account of the tone in Swift's "Digression on Madness" would be complete without reference to it. Without an attitude of melioration, no satire could be written, and this "Digression" is surely one of the great satires.

12

The Analysis of the Structure
of a Literary Work

S TRUCTURE in literary study may be defined as the organization of a literary work as influenced by its plot or main idea. The word is also sometimes defined as the pattern of emotions caused in the reader by the literary work. Though these two definitions are distinct, they are closely connected and under most circumstances are virtually inseparable. In imaginative works, structure refers to the chronological position of parts, scenes, episodes, chapters, and acts, and also to the logical or associational relationships among stanzas, ideas, images, or other divisions. In expository works, the word necessarily refers to the arrangement and development of ideas. Structure is a matter of the relationships among parts, usually described in terms of cause and effect, position in time, association, symmetry, and balance and proportion (the last two are usually concerned with evaluation, whereas the first three are more closely involved with description).

Literary artists universally aim at a unified impression in their works, and, because literature is a time art (it cannot be comprehended as a whole in one moment, as can a painting or a work of sculpture), the study of structure attempts to demonstrate that the idea and the arrangement of parts it causes add up to a total impression. You can see, therefore, that a study of structure is one avenue to the evaluation of literature, because a study of structure would bring out any lack of unity in a work and make that work subject to an adverse judgment, at least on these grounds.

In keeping with the second definition, it is also important to emphasize that structure may refer to the emotions in the reader. The aim of detective fiction, for example, is to produce the emotion of suspense in the reader; such fiction brings out this emotion by means of arousing related emotions, such as sympathy, fear, doubt (and therefore anxiety), and, finally, resolution of the suspense. Detective stories aim at producing these responses, and also play to a high degree upon the reader's curiosity. Similarly, many popular detective stories and westerns build strongly upon the feeling of indignation which is usually aroused by the criminal's committing some outrageous crime or unfairly taking advantage of the momentarily helpless hero. It might be added that indignation is a strong emotion in Milton's "Lycidas," although the reader is likely to feel doubt and uncertainty where Milton's speaker is expressing indignation. Much of the great poetry of Matthew Arnold is built upon the emotions of regret and nostalgia. The extent to which a modern reader can recreate these emotions usually determines his reactions toward poems like "The Scholar Gypsy" and "Stanzas from the Grand Chartreuse."

Emotions are also important in the structure of drama. The analysis of a typical play will uncover a *conflict,* but a full discussion of the play's structure should also be concerned with the tension caused by the conflict. One major idea in the Aristotelian analysis of tragedy is that tragedy aims at the purgation—catharsis—of pity and fear. In other words, Aristotle, in defining tragedy, was concerned with the proper arrangement of events in order to bring out these emotions in the audience, and this concern was mainly with the problem of structure.[1]

Examples, of course, could be multiplied. The important point, however, is that the study of structure is not confined exclusively to the physical placement of scenes, acts, episodes, etc. in the work under consideration. Structure is equally concerned with the logic and unity of a work and with the pattern of emotions aroused in the reader.

PURPOSE OF THE THEME ABOUT STRUCTURE

Your instructor's object in assigning a theme about the structure of a literary work is to help you become aware that form is essential to good literature, and that good literature cannot exist without form. The author you study was trying to create a work that would bring out not only the right incidents at the right time, but the right emotions in the reader. In analyzing the work for structure, you are attempting to show whether the author achieved his goals. The theme about structure therefore builds upon the theme about ideas in the literary work, for any analysis of structure must begin with the knowledge of the ideas and intentions of the work (see Chapter 5). In other words, the focus of your theme should be upon the *organization* of the work, but your emphasis should be upon the logic—the reasons—for this organization.

PROBLEMS

You will of course encounter problems in your theme about structure. You must interpret the idea of the work properly; and you must also

---

[1] *Poetics,* Ch. 14.

arrive at a sound conclusion about the work's effect. This problem is extremely subjective, but your interpretation will always be respected so long as it is reasonable.

Even more difficulty will be encountered when you attempt to relate your analysis and description of the parts in the work to your interpretation of the work's idea and effect. It is here that you must be especially careful. If your first judgment is that one part is not relevant, be sure that you have not missed some essential idea which would make it relevant. Make sure that your central idea is accurately comprehensive. One well-known writer, for example, stated that the last section of *Huckleberry Finn* is "just cheating." It seems apparent that his judgment resulted from an inadequate idea about the meaning of the novel. If he had considered that the novel contrasts common sense (Huck's idea of freeing Jim) with quixotism or faulty judgment (Tom's idea of freeing Jim with "style"), he would have modified his statement in keeping with this consideration.

You also have the usual problem of selectivity. What you choose to discuss will be made on the basis of your initial analysis of the idea and the effect of the work you analyze. A mere description of what happens in the work and where it happens is nothing more than summary. Your instructor is of course interested in your ability to describe the organization of the work, but he is much more interested in what you *make* out of your description. You must employ summary in your paper, but the summary must always be relevant to the point you are making about idea and effect. As always, your point is of primary importance, and should be kept foremost.

The form of your theme should take these matters into account.

THE ORGANIZATION OF YOUR THEME

Introduction

You should consider what you think is the most important idea in the work that you have analyzed, and you should also consider the principal emotional response on the part of the reader; make an attempt to relate these two. The problem here is finding the lowest common denominator that will take in all the principal events or statements in the work; you must make a general statement that is true for the work, and that therefore makes purposive all the events or statements in the work. Thus, a principal idea governing Milton's "Lycidas" is that life and effort have a final purpose (that life has meaning); a discussion of this idea would take into account the structure of the poem. Similarly, the main idea in Hemingway's *Farewell to Arms* is that happiness is not to be found on earth. Once you have arrived at an idea in this way, you should make it the central idea of your theme. Conclude your introduction with a thesis sentence.

Body

Work from your introduction into a discussion of the way in which the idea influences the form of the work. In this section you must describe the main parts of the work, showing the relationships among the parts. Use the central idea to show how all the various parts are dependent upon all the others (if the work is actually so well unified).

Conclusion

You should conclude your theme with an evaluation of the author's success so far as structure is concerned. Are all the parts of the work equally necessary? Do they occur in the best order? (A good test of this question is to ask yourself another: Would the work be damaged if any part were left out, or if any parts were transposed?) Are the parts successful in creating a total impression? If your answer to any of these questions is no, you have grounds for saying that the structure of the work is faulty. If your answer is always yes, you should probably conclude your theme with praise for the author, for you have been analyzing a perfectly unified work.

Sample Theme

An Analysis of the Structure of
"The Three Strangers" by Thomas Hardy

To me, Hardy's principal aim in "The Three Strangers" is to show the warm, kind, human qualities of the Wessex natives who are so prominent in the story. To bring out this human kindness, Hardy demonstrates the reactions of the natives to a series of incidents which clearly present a conflict between (1) duty toward law, and (2) duty toward a human being under condemnation of the law, whose crime has, in their eyes, been extenuated. In order to create a favorable impression that justice has been done and the eternal laws of humanity obeyed, Hardy utilizes the device of suspense: he thereby shows how the sympathies of the natives are favorably disposed toward humanity and the first stranger, and unfavorably disposed toward a punitive law and the second stranger. As he controls the attitudes of the natives, he controls the emotions of his readers in the same way. To make his case credible Hardy extensively describes not only the natives, but also the characteristics of the first two strangers. These are ambitious aims, which Hardy successfully achieves.

The opening one-fifth of the story is an introduction to the human kindness of the natives. The section moves from the big to the little— from the natural scenery surrounding Higher Crowstairs, to the general scene of humanity within the house, to the specific scene represented by Shepherd Fennel and his wife. Hardy is at great pains to show the perpetually human ways of the folk, not only in 182–, but by implication during all periods of human history. He makes the scene universal in his description of the dancing, which he describes in the words *apogee* and *perigee*. In other words, the dancing has been going on as long as the planets have been moving in their orbits. The incident the natives celebrate is the age-old one of birth and initiation into life (in this specific case, a christening). These people, Hardy suggests, are human beings uncontaminated by anything modern, for they have an "absolute confidence" in each other which begets "perfect ease," and which makes them immune from the modern poison of allowing business interests to interfere with friendship.[2] In short, this first section establishes contact with the folk and with their basic humanity—so strong a contact that it will not be lost during the remainder of the story. Clearly, the reader might assert, Hardy is going to make use of these human characteristics later on. This first section is therefore an effective introduction.

Against this backdrop, the second section builds suspense and offers the possibility of a false resolution. Covering slightly more than half of the story, this section introduces suspense in the persons of the three strangers and the actions in which they are engaged. Though throughout the section a person might lose focus on the natives, it must be emphasized that Hardy's real purpose in bringing in the strangers is to illustrate his main idea that the natives are kind and human. Each of the strangers is mysterious, though Hardy resolves the mystery of the second stranger almost immediately. Of the three strangers, the first is characterized by his likeableness, his desire to remain anonymous, his lack of tobacco, and his taking a weapon when the second knock on the door is heard. The second stranger is of course the hangman, whom Hardy causes the natives, and the reader, to dislike. The third stranger is not developed at all, except that the section closes with the idea that he is the escaped criminal. Momentarily, therefore, attention is drawn away from the mystery surrounding the first stranger, since the third is actually a red herring. The second section therefore concludes on a note of suspense.

The third section, the last quarter of the story, brings out the events leading up to the resolution of the suspense caused by our desire to know the identities of the first and third strangers. In a comic scene

---

[2] *Short Stories for Study*, 3rd ed., Raymond W. Short and Richard B. Sewall, eds. (New York: Holt, Rinehart & Winston, Inc., 1956), p. 108. All page numbers refer to this edition.

the natives search for and capture the third stranger, who then informs his captors that the first stranger, and not himself, is the escaped criminal. At this point Hardy demonstrates that his story all along has been building up to the reaction of the natives when they learn this fact. The knowledge forces them into a decision, which they tacitly make "on the side of the fugitive," since they feel that "the intended punishment was cruelly disproportioned to the transgression" (p. 131). After this climax—the human decision of the natives—the story quickly ends.

The total effect of Hardy's structure, therefore, belies the expectations aroused by the title, and a casual reader might feel that Hardy has cluttered his story with too much detail about the natives. But more consideration shows that the action concerning the three strangers exists in order to bring out the warm humanity of the natives, and that the story, just like all stories, is finally about the entire society in which it occurs. In this case, Hardy suggests, or implies, that the story is as old as the race.

His use of suspense supports my claim. He deliberately avoids saying until the very end that the first stranger is the escaped sheep-stealer, although his hints about this fact at second sight are very obvious. In this way, he builds up sympathy for the stranger, and avoids our forming an early, purely legal reaction against him until all the facts are in. Because of this delay in our knowledge, we form our opinions about the stranger *as a human being* and *not* as a criminal. And, since our opinion is formed along with that of the natives, we become sympathetic toward their decision to neglect the strict letter of the law in favor of the more compelling human obligation, particularly in view of the obnoxious and severe character of the law as personified by the hangman. Hardy wants no enduring suspense about the harshness and injustice represented by this second, horrid figure who delights in his ghoulish work.

Hardy therefore ends his story just as he began it, on the notes of (a) the overwhelming need for human kindness and (b) the permanence of life, in which birth and death are cycles. Thereby, he has created a unified structure with a total impression similar to the one occasioned by his statement about the life of the folk, the natives, in his poem "In Time of 'The Breaking of Nations' ":

> Yet this will go onward the same
> Though Dynasties pass.

13

The Prosodic Analysis of Poetry

*P*ROSODY is the word commonly used in reference to the study of sound and rhythm in poetry. Though sound and rhythm are the primary concern of prosodic study, however, these elements are never to be discussed in a vacuum; they are always an integral part of every good poem, and are important only as they are related to the other parts. *Prosody* is the general word referring to sound and rhythm, but other, equally descriptive, words are *metrics, versification, mechanics of verse,* and *numbers* (*numbers* is not common at present, but it was current in Pope's time. Longfellow also used it). Some persons call sound and rhythm the *music* of poetry. Whatever term your instructor might use, then, he means the study of sound and rhythm in poetry.

Your instructor will usually ask you to write a theme about prosody in order to give you the opportunity (a) to develop your sensitivity to the poet's language *as sound,* and (b) to become aware of the relationship of sound and rhythm to content. You will realize, as you make your analysis and write your theme, that the poet devoted much of his creative energy not only to the content of his poem, but equally to the manner of conveying his content. This assignment will help you to become a more skilled reader, better equipped to define poetry and analyze sounds. You should also have an additional standard by which to measure the quality of poems. In short, this assignment should deepen your appreciation of a poet's achievement.

Many students, having accustomed themselves to paying attention only to the ideas and events in prose works, approach a theme on prosody with much apprehension. They feel either that the study of prosody is barren, devoid of content, or that they cannot do this sort of job because they have never done it before. But the study of prosody is not barren, and there is no more reason for timidity on this assignment than on any other. With knowledge of a few terms and concepts, together with close attention to a poem, you can do a good job. There is much pleasure to be gained from analyzing a poem like Donne's "Batter My Heart," and from seeing that his style is in complete accord with his meaning. When you come to this realization you have actually encountered the living mind of the poet at work, selecting words and arranging rhythms not just by accident but by premeditated design and masterly control. You cannot appreciate poetry fully until you know something about prosody.

Your main problem in this assignment is to develop the vocabulary for discussing what you, and every sensitive reader, can perceive. In essence, your job is to translate the written poem into the spoken poem, and then to describe the noteworthy and outstanding characteristics of the sounds. Fortunately, the study of metrics has provided you with a ready-made vocabulary for discussing what you hear. Much of your preparation for this assignment will therefore be simply to learn the vocabulary and apply it.

POETRY AND PROSE: RHYTHM

Poetry is difficult to define exactly. It is like prose in that it employs words to convey thoughts and impressions and to tell stories, but prose is expansive—its content is characterized by the use of examples which are usually developed at some length. In addition, prose is relatively unemotional. As a result your voice, when you read a prose passage, tends to remain within a rather narrow range of pitch; the accents and lengths of the individual words are submerged. Poetry is usually more demanding. It is more compact and more intense in its expression, and the poet consequently devotes a special care to the sounds and rhythms of words and lines. When you read poetry, therefore, you must give particular attention to individual words; your units of expression will be shorter; your voice will go through a wider range of pitch. The reading of poetry generally requires more vocal activity than the reading of prose; this additional activity is a direct result of poetry's greater compactness and intensity.

POETRY AND PROSE: SOUND

Just as poetry pays particular attention to rhythm, it requires special emphasis upon the sounds of individual words. You are likely to read prose by sentence lengths, minimizing the sounds of words as you emphasize the ideas in the text. But in reading poetry you might frequently linger over sounds, if they seem to have been intended for that purpose by the poet. Imagine reading these lines, for example, without making your listeners conscious of the *s, l, m,* and *w* consonant sounds, and of the *short ĭ, short ŏ,* and *short ŭ* vowel sounds:

> And more, to lulle him in his slumber soft,
>   A trickling streame from high rocke tumbling downe

> And ever-drizling raine upon the loft,
> Mixt with a murmuring winde, much like the sowne
> Of swarming Bees, did cast him in a swowne:
>   —Spenser, *Faerie Queene*, Canto I, Stanza 41

Try reading aloud the passage of prose you are now looking at; linger over some of the sounds; give your voice a similarly wide range of pitch. Perhaps the effect of this overreading will make you aware of some of the differences between poetry and prose. Poetry—unlike prose—invites intensive, energetic reading because of its compact, intense nature. If you can perceive these facts, you must realize that poets also have this objective in mind. You can therefore see that a study of rhythm and sound is an integral part of poetic study.

VARIOUS DEMANDS UPON THE SOUND OF POETRY

From the discussion thus far, you can realize that there are three main elements which must be considered in prosodic analysis. These are *rhetoric and emotion, sound,* and *rhythm.* All are equally important, and all act at the same moment in any given poem.

Rhetoric and Emotion

First and foremost is the rhetorical and emotional demand. Because poetry is an art of communication through words, the poet will necessarily wish to create emphasis by arranging his phrases, sentences, and paragraphs in the most effective way. As this arrangement must affect the levels of pitch and stress, and will affect the placement of pauses, the rhetorical demand is sometimes in agreement with, and sometimes at odds with, the formal rhythm of the poem, depending upon the poet's will.

Also a part of the rhetorical demand is the arrangement of words into *cadence groups.* You might regard these groups as the rhythm of words resulting from their being put into phrases. In the following lines, for example, the words tend to bunch together into groups separated by extremely slight pauses:

> Into the deep reaches of that dimly lit sea
> Our spray-cased craft rammed a pathless way.

The words *Into the deep reaches* make a group of six syllables which belong together by virtue of being an adverb phrase. Similarly, *Our spray-cased craft* forms a noun group. These groups form their own indissoluble rhythmical unit that may or may not correspond to the formal, regular, or metrical demands of the poem. The kind of poetry known as *free verse* tends to make cadence groups more important than meter.

The role of emotion in poems deserves special consideration when you study prosody. Depending upon the emotions demanded by a poem, you may raise or lower your voice, increase or decrease the speed of your pronunciation, accentuate or minimize certain sounds, and pause heavily or lightly after certain words. Emotion, in short, affects the expression with which you read a poem or passage. You can describe the effects of emotion in prosody to the extent that it affects pitch, stress, length, and pause, but you will probably find that the various tones of voice and the subtle shades of spoken expression are very difficult to describe in your theme.

Sound

You must consider the sounds of the words themselves, both independently and as they influence each other in their order in the lines. The sounds of speech have been classified by modern students of language as "segmental." The good poet puts words together so that their sounds will augment his meaning, not contradict it. In other words, the poet can use the *sounds* of his words as a form of expression in addition to the dictionary meanings of the words. He may use words containing recurring patterns of sounds in order to make your ear conscious of the poem's unity. Sometimes he may even use words containing sounds that are actually reminiscent of the things he is describing, as in the conclusion of the passage from Tennyson analyzed in the sample theme.

Rhythm

Another important element is the rhythm of the words when arranged into lines of poetry. The rhythm of English is usually determined by the relationship of heavily stressed to less heavily stressed syllables.[1] In pronouncing words you give some syllables more force (loudness) than others. For convenience, you may call the syllables to which you give more force *heavily stressed,* and those to which you give less force *lightly stressed.* In most English poetry the poet has regularized the heavily and lightly stressed syllables into patterns called *feet.* He usually fills his lines with a specific number of the same feet, and that number determines the *meter* of the line. Frequently rhetorical needs lead him to substitute other feet

---

[1] Martin Halpern has challenged this traditional view by claiming that in iambic verse, for example, stress alone is not the only element determining feet, but that pitch and length are equally important. If one holds this position he will discover less substitution in English poetry than if he maintains the traditional view, but he will also discover greater variety within the limits of the foot. See "On the Two Chief Metrical Modes in English," *PMLA,* LXXVII (1962), 177–186.

for the regular feet. Whether there is *substitution* or not, however, the number and kind of feet in each line constitute the meter of that line. Notice that the major influence here is number; that is, you measure English verse by the division of syllables according to degrees of stress.

The complex interaction of all these various demands produces what we commonly call the sounds and rhythms of a poem, and the prosodic interest created by any poem depends upon the degrees of tension produced by the various demands. If all the demands were perfectly in accord, the result would be perfect regularity, and very soon perfect boredom. In most poetry, however, each of the elements has a certain degree of independence, thereby producing effects of variation and tension. Variation is a strong cause of interest and beauty, and tension promotes interest and emotional involvement in a poem. An understanding of prosody is important in the evaluation of poetry because sound and rhythm are important in the structural and emotional complex that is poetry.

MINIMUM REQUIREMENTS FOR CONSIDERING SOUNDS IN POETRY

Though you have been speaking the language for many years, the chances are great that you have not systematically studied the sounds that you utter daily. For this reason you must be sure, before you undertake a prosodic analysis, that you have a basic approach to the analysis of sound.

Sounds are usually divided into *vowel sounds* (including *semivowels*) and *consonant sounds*. It is important to emphasize the word *sound* as distinguished from the letters of the alphabet, for often the same letters represent different sounds. You should have some acceptable notational system for indicating sounds. Perhaps the most readily available systems of pronunciation are in the collegiate dictionaries; these systems, which have won fairly wide acceptance, take into account regional differences in pronunciation. If you have questions about syllabication and the position of stresses, you can use the dictionary as an authority. Two other systems of indicating sounds are based upon more recent scientific analyses. The first is the *International Phonetic Alphabet* as adapted for use in English, and the second is a system called *phonemic*.[2] The great virtue of these notational systems is that they are more descriptive than those in the dic-

---

[2] For the adapted phonetic alphabet see Samuel Moore, *Historical Outlines of English Sounds and Inflections,* Revised by Albert H. Marckwardt (Ann Arbor: George Wahr Publishing Co., 1962), pp. 8–18. For the phonemic system see Donald J. Lloyd and Harry R. Warfel, *American English in its Cultural Setting* (New York: Alfred A. Knopf, 1956), pp. 294–318.

tionaries. The phonemic system is especially useful because it presents a satisfactory method for analyzing not only sounds, but also pauses and pitches. Because the dictionary systems are readily available, however, they will be used in the following discussion.

Vowel Sounds and Their Qualities

There are two systems operating in the pronunciation of vowel sounds. The first is *front-central-back,* and the second is *high-mid-low.* These terms depend upon the position of the tongue during the pronunciation of a vowel sound. For your analysis of prosody, you need to consider only the extremes of *high-front* and *low-back.* Observe that the vowel sounds *ē, ĭ, ā,* are all produced in a narrow space between the tongue and the hard palate. These sounds are both *front* and *high.* By contrast, pronounce the *ä* in *arm.* Notice that your tongue is still in a front position, but that it has dropped far down in your mouth. This *ä,* in other words, is a *low front* vowel sound. Now pronounce the vowel sound *ō* as in *coal.* Notice that your tongue has stayed high, but has dropped *back* in your throat. The *ō* sound is a *high, back,* and *rounded* sound. Now pronounce the *ô in orphan,* and the *ōō* in *troop.* Notice that these are both *back* and *low rounded* sounds.

To a considerable degree, the context in which a word appears governs the pitch and intensity of the sounds in that word. Briefly, however, the low, back sounds tend to be lower in pitch than the front, high sounds. For this reason, though the sounds themselves are neutral in meaning, they can be used by poets to augment light (high front) or heavy (low back) effects. A remarkable example of the combination of high-front and low-back vowel sounds is this couplet from Pope, which demonstrates an interweaving of front *ā* and *ē* sounds through back *ō, ä,* and *ōō* sounds, just as the river which Pope describes would weave through the cold wasteland:

> Lo where Maotis sleeps, and hardly flows
> The freezing Thanais through a waste of snows.
>   —*Dunciad,* III, 87–88

Semivowel Sounds

The semivowels are *w, y,* and *h.* A semivowel is sometimes used in conjunction with a vowel sound at the end of an open syllable (e.g., go = gow; weigh = way). At other times the semivowel has the appearance of a consonant (e.g., *w*innowing *w*ind; *u*nion; *h*aven [but the *h* in *h*onor is silent]). The semivowels are not often used for heavy, explosive effects (though the *h* and the *k* sounds are not very different).

Consonant Sounds

Consonant sounds themselves are meaningless unless they are put into a context. The *s*, for example, in a context of rage, can augment the rage, but in a quiet context it can produce a drowsy, sleepy effect (see the earlier example from Spenser).

When discussing consonant sounds, you must be especially aware of the differences between the letters themselves and the sounds they represent. Thus, *t*rip, *t*his, na*t*ion, *t*hrough, moun*t*ain, Be*tt*y, all have the letter *t*, but the spoken sounds are all different. *S*weet, *s*hrove, and flow*s* all have *s*'s, but these *s*'s represent different sounds.

RHYME AND METER

Once you have acquired a method for analyzing and describing sounds, you can go on to the analysis of rhyme and meter.

Rhyme

Rhyme, which refers to the recurrence of identical sounds—usually in words ending lines (e.g., t*ime* and ch*ime*)—is the most easily recognized characteristic of poetry. When you describe a rhyme scheme, you should use letters (i.e., *a, b, c,* etc.). Each new letter indicates a new sound; a repeated letter indicates a rhyme. In a Shakespearean sonnet, for example, the rhyme scheme is *abab cdcd efef gg*. The rhyme scheme of an Italian or Petrarchan sonnet is *abba abba cd cd cd*.

Whenever rhyme occurs you should analyze its effects and the way these are achieved. Observe the grammatical forms of the rhyming words. If a poet rhymes only nouns, for example, his rhymes are likely to be monotonous, for he should show some variety in the grammatical forms. You should also observe, if masculine rhyme is the norm, whether there are feminine or other rhymes, and the effect of these. Another area of study is whether the rhymes are unusual or surprising. If a poet relied on "sure returns of still expected rhymes" (like the *breeze* blowing through the *trees*), his rhymes would be obvious and dull. Observe that in the following couplet by Byron the rhyming words are verbs, and that wit and surprise result from the riddle in the first line and the meaning of the final word:

> 'Tis strange—the Hebrew noun which means "I am,"
> The English always use to govern d--n.
> —*Don Juan,* I, xiv, 111–112

Although few rhymes will provide the humor of this one, you should observe the method of rhyming in the poems you study. As you make further analyses you will be impressed with the way in which your understanding of the craft of poetry will grow.

In connection with rhyme the following terms are important. In *eye rhyme* or *sight rhyme* the rhyming words look the same, but are pronounced differently (e.g., "I *wind*" and "I am frozen by the *wind*"). In *slant rhyme* the rhyming vowel sounds are different in quality while the consonant sounds are identical (e.g., *could* and solit*ude*). Frequently the rhythm of a rhyme is important, and for this reason you should know the terms *masculine rhyme* (the rhyme of words on accented syllables, e.g., fl*ows*, sn*ows*), *feminine rhyme* (a rhyming trochee, e.g., *see one* and *be one;* fant*astic* and el*astic*), and *triple rhyme* (a rhyming dactyl, e.g., *easily*, br*eezily*). Masculine rhyme is ordinarily used for serious purposes, whereas feminine and triple rhyme lend themselves easily to comic effects.

Meter

Meter is the systematic regulation of poetic rhythm. In order to discover the prevailing metrical system in any poem, you *scan* that poem. The act of scanning is called *scansion.*

Your first problem in scansion is to recognize where syllables are and to distinguish one syllable from another. Experience has shown that students who in the early grades have been taught to read by the "word-recognition" method, as contrasted with the "syllable" method, often find it hard to distinguish syllables. This difficulty is unfortunate, because an understanding of syllables is the first requirement in the feeling for rhythms in poetry. You must therefore be especially cautious, and realize that words like *merrier* and *terrier,* for example, are three-syllable words, as is *solitude;* another three-syllable combination is *dial hand.* If you find difficulty in perceiving the syllables in lines of poetry, a good idea is to read each word aloud separately, pronouncing every syllable, before reading the words in poetic context. The practice of reading poetry aloud is good in any event. If you have been encouraged to read for speed, you must abandon this approach when you read poetry.

The next step in preparation for your theme is to interpret *stress* or *accent.* You are concerned to show the syllables that receive major and light emphasis, and you need a system for showing these syllables. In scansion a heavy or primary accent is commonly indicated by an acute accent mark or slash (/), while a light accent may be indicated by a circle or zero (o). There is no reason for absoluteness in this system, however, for your instructor might direct you to indicate heavy accents by an upright line (|) or a horizontal (—), and weak or light syllables by a horizontal

(—), a cross (x), or a half circle (◡). As with the determination of the number of syllables in a line you must, when you read aloud, listen carefully to hear which syllables are heavily stressed and which are lightly stressed. If you are ever in doubt, use the dictionary and the stress given there. For example, the pronunciation of the word *indeciduous* is shown as follows in the *American College Dictionary*:

$$\text{in}\,\overset{/}{\text{di}}\,\overset{/}{\text{sij}}\,\text{oo}\,\text{əs}$$

A light accent mark is placed over *in,* while *sij* receives a heavier accent mark. The other syllables are lightly stressed. If you found a line of poetry in which this word appeared, then, you would scan it as follows:

$$\overset{\circ}{\text{The}}\,\overset{/}{\text{in}}\,\text{- / }\,\overset{\circ}{\text{de}}\,\text{- }\,\overset{/}{\text{cid-}}\,\text{/ }\,\overset{\circ\circ}{\text{u-ous}}\,\overset{/}{\text{trees}}\,\text{/ spring}\,\overset{\frown}{\text{forth.}}$$

Although the demands of the poetic line may lessen the force of a heavily-stressed syllable in relation to other words in the line, you will seldom be mistaken if you rely upon the dictionary.

There is a problem in determining accent because some stresses are stronger than others, and some lightly-accented syllables are stressed more than others. In fact, modern linguists have recognized three degrees of major stress. The first is *primary, major,* or *heavy,* indicated by an acute accent (/). The second is *secondary* or *medium,* shown by a circumflex accent (∧). The third is *tertiary* or *light,* marked by a grave accent (\).[3] It seems obvious that you should recognize these differences when you scan poetry. A line like the following, by Ben Jonson, can be scanned as regular iambic pentameter:

$$\overset{\circ}{\text{If}}\,\overset{/}{\text{thou}}\,\text{/ }\,\overset{\circ}{\text{wouldst}}\,\overset{/}{\text{know}}\,\text{/ }\,\overset{\circ}{\text{the}}\,\overset{/}{\text{vir}}\,\text{- / }\,\overset{\circ}{\text{tues}}\,\overset{/}{\text{of}}\,\text{/ }\,\overset{\circ}{\text{man-}}\overset{/}{\text{kind.}}$$

The syllables *wouldst, tues,* and *man* are all lightly stressed according to the demands of meter (see below), yet you can feel that these syllables should receive heavier emphasis than *the* and even the word *of* (*of* is a major stress according to the meter). Similarly, *thou, know,* and *virtues* accumulate stress, so that the heaviest accent of the three falls on *vir,* just as *virtues* contains the climax of the idea of the line. Yet by what the acute accent indicates, *thou, know,* and *vir* all seem to receive the same emphasis as *of.* How can you indicate these differences when you make your scansion?

If you feel confident enough of your perceptions, you might attempt to use the acute, circumflex, and grave accents to show differences among the various heavily-stressed syllables. If your ear is not highly trained,

---

[3] See Lloyd and Warfel, *op. cit.,* p. 315, or W. Nelson Francis, *The Structure of American English* (New York: Ronald Press Co., 1958), p. 153.

however, a more likely compromise is to use the acute accent for the heaviest major stresses, and the grave accent for less heavy major stresses. Thus, the line by Jonson might be scanned as follows:

> If thou / wouldst know / the vir - / tues of / man-kind.

Let us see how the opening line of Shakespeare's *Henry V* might be marked:

> O! for / a Muse / of fire / that would / as - cend . . .

If you do not use this system, but employ only the acute accent and the circle, be sure, in your theme, to show your awareness that not all heavy stresses are equal.

Since discussion of rhythm could be endless, you should know at least the following. Rhythm in poetry is usually considered in terms of metrical *feet*. In English, the most important feet are:

1. *Iamb.* A light followed by a heavy stress. The iamb is the most common foot in English. (*be - have*).
2. *Trochee.* A heavy accent followed by a light (*u - nit*).
3. *Dactyl.* A heavy followed by two lights (*might - i - est*).
4. *Anapaest.* Two lights followed by a heavy (*for a Muse*).
5. *Imperfect Foot.* A single syllable; (/) by itself, or (o) by itself.
6. *Pyrrhic.* Two unstressed syllables, as in *like a* / great ring.
7. *Spondee.* Two heavy accents, as in *great ring*. A noticeable way to show the spondee is to connect the two syllables with a mark like a corporal's *chevrons*, as is done here. Spondees seem to give special difficulty in prosodic analysis. A principal reason is that quite often *pitch* is confused with *stress*, as in the following example:

> Such seems / your beau- / ty still.

Though *beauty still* may easily be spoken at one pitch, there is a definite weakening of stress over the *y*, so that *beauty* is definitely not a spondee. Similarly, in "Three winters cold," the syllables *three* and *win* are of equal, heavy stress, and should therefore be marked as a spondee; but *ters* and *cold* are not equal, since *ters*, as a part of *winters*, receives a weak stress.

Another problem with spondees occurs if they are mistaken for pyrrhic feet. A spondee is the juxtaposition of two syllables of equally *heavy* stress, not of equally *light* stress.

8. *Amphibrach.* A light, heavy, and light. *The chestnut; susurrus.* This foot is not common, though in the line "Such seems your beauty still," some people could argue that *your beauty* is properly an amphibrach, followed by an imperfect foot (*still*). Amphibrachs may be seen in the opening line of the song "The Old Oaken Bucket":

ŏ ╱ ŏ ŏ ╱ ŏ ŏ ╱ ŏ̄ ŏ ╱ ŏ
How dear to / my heart are / the scenes of / my childhood.

9. *Amphimac.* A heavy, light, and heavy. *Made a way; having fun.* The amphimac is not at all common; most rhythms of this sort can be explained by reference to the more common feet.

POETIC DEVICES

After you have finished your scansion, you should study the poem in order to discover any poetic devices employed by the poet. The common ones follow.

Assonance

In connection with vowel sounds you should become familiar with *assonance,* which is the employment in close quarters of identical vowel sounds in different words (e.g., sw*i*ft Cam*i*lla sk*i*ms). Be cautious, however, about equating sounds like the $\overset{\shortmid}{e}$ in d*e*ceived with the $\bar{e}$ in tr*ee*; the $\overset{\shortmid}{e}$ in *de* is not a true long $\bar{e}$, but instead is a half-long $\overset{\shortmid}{e}$, and some would maintain that it is a *schwa* (a sound like the *a* in *sofa*). Also, you should not select isolated instances of a sound in your description of assonance. If, for example, you find three words in the same line that include a long *ā* sound, these form a pattern and are worthy of mention as an instance of assonance; *but,* if you find a word six lines later that includes a long *ā*, this word should not be mentioned as part of the pattern. The word is too far away from the pattern to be significant.

Devices Caused by Consonant Sounds

The most common devices in poetry employing consonant sounds are these:

ALLITERATION, which is the repetition of similar or identical consonant sounds beginning syllables in relatively close patterns, e.g., "La*b*orious, heavy, *b*usy, *b*old, and *b*lind," and "While *p*ensive *p*oets *p*ainful vigils keep." Used sparingly, alliteration gives strength to a poem by emphasizing key words, but too much can cause comic effects.

CONSONANCE, which differs from alliteration by the repetition of two or more identical consonant sounds, e.g., li*v*e, lea*v*e; g*r*oaned, g*r*ound; to*p*, ti*p*; g*r*ab, g*r*ub, etc. This device does not occur very often in most of the poems you will encounter, for it calls attention to itself, and might detract from an important idea.

OTHER CONSONANT PATTERNS   Frequently a poet may repeat identical or similar consonant sounds which, while not beginning syllables, create a pattern and thereby have prosodic importance, e.g., "In the*se* places freezing breezes easily cause sneezes." (In this example both *s* and *z* are sounded as *z;* such a pattern is hard to overlook.) In "The *pebbles* in the *bubbling pool*," both *p* and *b* are *labial* consonant sounds (i.e., they are made by a momentary stoppage of breath at the lips); *p* is a *voiceless* stopped sound, whereas *b* is a *voiced* stopped sound. Because of the similarity, the two sounds should be mentioned as part of a pattern.

ONOMATOPOEIA Onomatopoeia is a blend of consonant and vowel sounds with rhythm to create the effect of imitating the sound of the thing being described. Onomatopoeia is technically difficult to achieve because it depends almost entirely upon context (some rare instances of onomatopoeic words like *buzz* being excepted), but it is powerful when it occurs. For example, at the end of the passage from Tennyson's *Morte D'Arthur* which is analyzed in the sample theme, a lake is mentioned. Because our minds are therefore directed toward the image of a lake, the *l* sounds (which, along with *r* sounds, are frequently called "liquids") may be taken to suggest the sounds of waves lapping against a shore. This combination of sense and sound is onomatopoeia.

PAUSE AND EMPHASIS: OTHER MEANS OF POETIC EFFECT

Pause (Caesura)

Spoken speech is composed of groups of syllables forming intelligible units, separated by pauses which add to the intelligibility. In poetry, the pause is called a *caesura* or *cut*. In this line by Ben Jonson, for example, there are two pauses, or *caesurae:*

> Thou art not, *Penshurst,* built to envious show.

The first caesura follows *not* and the second follows *Penshurst.* In the following line by Pope there are three caesurae:

> His actions', passions', being's, use and end.

You can see that poets arrange pauses judiciously in order to make their lines interesting, varied, and emphatic. In your prosodic analysis, you should therefore make observations about the use of caesura in the poem you analyze.

The caesura is best indicated by two diagonal lines (//) in order to distinguish it from the single diagonal lines separating feet. For most purposes these two diagonals are all you need. However, there are subtle distinctions among caesurae, and as you develop your ear you will perceive these distinctions. A pause before which the voice is not raised, such as the one between *Penshurst* and *built,* might best be shown by the two diagonal bars (//). The pause between *O* and *for* in *O! for a Muse* is also of this nature, because the pause indicates that there is more immediately to follow. But the pause at the end of a declarative sentence is different, as it usually follows a lowering of *pitch* and is therefore a definite means by which the end of a statement is indicated. Perhaps these caesurae, usually marked by a period or semicolon in the poem, could be marked by three diagonals (///). Then too, there is still a different caesura that immediately follows the elevation of pitch that usually indicates a question. This type might conveniently be marked with a double reverse diagonal (\\).

Emphasis

PITCH AND LENGTH   Pitch and length are two of the most important elements in effective expression. So far as pitch indicates meaning through the raising and lowering of the voice before pauses, it can be fairly well analyzed and discussed. More difficult, however, and far more subtle, is the raising and lowering of the voice that occurs because of the dramatic requirements of a poem, or because of the need for keeping the voice interestingly modulated. This variation is subjective to the extent that it is not properly a part of essential, denotative meaning, but for the most part the poetry you read will demand various levels of pitch. If a reader is at all sensitive, he cannot read poetry at the same vocal level.

Demanding similar alertness is the perception of length or *quantity*. Length is in an anomalous position in the scansion of English poetry, since it does not determine the formation of metrical feet. But length is certainly important in the sensitive reading of poetry, and you should be aware of it.

Length is inherent in the long vowel sounds, as in the words *all, raid, reed, red, road, broad, food,* and *bird*. Any of these words preceded by a word containing a short vowel sound forms an iamb (e.g., *the road*), but if two of them are together, they cause a spondee (e.g., *the broad road*). Shorter vowels can be seen in the words *bat, bet, bit, bought, but, foot,* and *the*.

Though the lengths of vowels in particular words are relatively fixed, the poet can create greater or lesser lengths by the ways in which he uses words in context. Notice, for example, how Shakespeare controls length in these lines by the careful selection of words:

> . . . and then my state,
> Like to the lark at break of day arising
> From sullen earth, sing hymns at heaven's gate.

> —Sonnet 29, lines 10–12

As contrasted with the lengthened $\bar{a}$ of *day*, the vowel sounds in *like, lark,* and *break* are restrained by the voiceless consonant stop *k*. The greatest skill, however, is shown in the way the passage (and the entire sonnet) builds toward the phrase *sings hymns*, which contains short $\breve{i}$ vowel sounds lengthened by the nasal consonant sounds *ng* and *m* (both of which are lengthened by the voiced continuous consonant sound *z*). As the poem reaches its climax in the image, the sound also reaches its climax. There are few more glorious experiences in English poetry than reading these lines, and the cause cannot be explained by resort only to stress. The principal cause, in the context, is length.

Needless to say, the most skillful prosodists are able to make the matters of pitch and length infallibly right, while lesser poets cannot control them. As you read more and more good poetry, your awareness of pitch and length will improve. A good way to hasten this improvement is to read poetry aloud, and read it aloud frequently. If it helps you, try to act out the situation of the poem as you read.

When you make your first prosodic analysis, your instructor will probably not expect much from you in the analysis of pitch and length, but as you progress in your study of poetry you should be able to indicate your perceptions in your themes. One of the marks of your increasing understanding and appreciation of poetry (and also of your ability to write about it) will be your growing awareness of pitch and length.

EMPHASIS ACHIEVED BY METRICAL VARIATION, REAL AND APPARENT   Most poems are written in a pattern that can readily be perceived. Thus Shakespeare's plays usually follow the pattern of *blank verse* (unrhymed iambic pentameter) and Milton's *Paradise Lost* follows this same pattern. Such a pattern is no more than a rhythmical norm, however. For interest and emphasis (and perhaps because of the very nature of the English language) the norm is varied by the *substitution* of other feet for the normal feet and also by the effect of such substitution.

The following line is from the "January" eclogue of Spenser's *Shepherd's Calendar*. Though the abstract pattern of the line is iambic pentameter, it is varied by the substitution of two other feet:

All in / a sun - / shine day, / as did / be - fall.

In the first foot, *All in* is a trochee, and *shine day* is a spondee. This line shows real substitution.

Many poets, however, create the effect of substitution by a means which we shall call apparent variation. An outstanding example of this variation in an iambic pentameter line is this one by Pope:

His ac - / tions', // pas - / sions', // be - / ing's, // use / and end;

Ordinarily there is one caesura in a line of this type, but in this one there
are three, each one of which produces a strong pause. The line is regularly iambic, and should be scanned as regular. But in reading, the effect
is different. Because of the pauses, which occur in the middles of the
second, third, and fourth feet, the line is actually read as an amphibrach,
a trochee, a trochee, an imperfect foot, and a regular iamb. Though lines
like this one are regular, the practical effect—the apparent effect—is of
variation and tension. In this well-known line from Shakespeare, apparent
variation may also be seen:

If music be the food of love, play on!

This line is regularly iambic except, perhaps, for a spondee in *play on,*
but the reading of the line conflicts with the normative pattern. Thus,
If music may be read as an amphibrach and *be the food* is in practice an
anapaest. Because of the subordinate clause, the caesura does not come
until after the eighth syllable. These apparent variations produce the
effect of natural, ordinary speech, because Shakespeare has lavished a good
deal of his art upon the line.

In whatever poetry you study, your main concern in noting variation
is to observe the abstract metrical pattern, and then to note the variations on this pattern—real and apparent—and the principal causes for
these variations. By analyzing these causes you will greatly enhance your
understanding of the poet's craft.

EMPHASIS CAUSED BY TENSION BETWEEN SENTENCE STRUCTURE AND LINES
The basic working units of expression in prose are phrases, clauses, and
sentences. The same applies to poetry, with the added complexity that
metrical demands frequently conflict with these units. Some poets (e.g.,
Milton, Chaucer, Wordsworth) create emphasis and tension in their poetry
by making strong demands for sentence structure over and against an
established metrical pattern. Here, for example, is a short passage from
Wordsworth, laid out as prose:

> And I have felt a presence that disturbs me with the joy of elevated
> thoughts; a sense sublime of something far more deeply interfused, whose
> dwelling is the light of setting suns, and the round ocean and the living
> air, and the blue sky, and in the mind of man.
>
> —"Tintern Abbey," lines 93–99

It is difficult, though not impossible, to perceive the actual line divisions
in this example. In other words, Wordsworth is superimposing an extended sentence structure upon the metrical structure, a characteristic
habit that is perfectly in keeping with meditative or philosophic poetry.
Similarly, Milton is famous for his extended verse paragraphs in blank
verse.

Other poets, by contrast, blend their sentence structure almost completely into their rhythmical pattern. Take, for example, this passage from Pope, which is also laid out as prose:

> Nor public flame, nor private, dares to shine; nor human spark is left, nor glimpse divine! Lo! thy dread empire, Chaos, is restored; light dies before thy uncreating word: thy hand, great Anarch! lets the curtain fall; and universal darkness buries all.
>
> —*Dunciad*, IV, 651–656

The sentences are perfectly fitted to the lines, making the counting of feet comparatively easy, and we could determine the length of each line easily, without the aid of the rhyme. As a result, Pope and poets like him have frequently been accused of too much "boring regularity," whereas poets like Wordsworth and Milton have been praised for their greater "freedom." In actuality, however, the principles of variation are used by all these poets, with Wordsworth and Milton adding extensive syntactic variation to metrical variations.

You should know the technical terms connected with these variations. If a pause occurs at the end of the line, that line is called *end-stopped:*

> A thing of beauty is a joy forever:

But if the line has no punctuation mark and runs over into the next line, it is called *run-on.* The term used to describe run-on lines is *enjambment:*

> Its loveliness increases; it will never
> Pass into nothingness; but still will keep
> A bower quiet for us, and a sleep
> Full of sweet dreams, . . .
>
> —Keats, "Endymion," lines 1–5

THE ORGANIZATION OF YOUR THEME

You should attempt to show the operation of all these component elements of poetry. Your theme should contain the following parts:

Introduction

This section should include a brief discussion of the rhetorical or dramatic situation of the poem as it leads into a consideration of prosody. That is, is the poem narrative or expository in structure? Is there a speaker? Who is he? What are his characteristics? What situation is described? What special poetic theories are apparently being exemplified in the passage? What is the principal idea of the passage? What is the dominant mood of the poem? The object of answering questions like these (you do not need to answer all of them, and may want to ask others) is to make possible the evaluation of how well the prosody of the passage lives up to the expectations aroused by the rhetorical or dramatic situation. Discussion of these questions is therefore very important. As a structural device in your themes, the discussion will give more purpose and logic to the technical discussion to follow (the introductory discussion will also help you in your prosodic analysis of the poem or passage).

Body

Here you should discuss the rhythm of the passage. You ought to discuss the basic metrical pattern and variations upon it (and where the variations occur). You ought also to discuss the relationships of the syntactic (word order) units to the meter. Is there conflict between the two? If so, why might this conflict exist? Do you see any evidence of the poet's design therein? What is the ultimate effect of the conflict? Does it seem to be appropriate to the rhetorical situation? If there is agreement between the sentence structure and the metrical emphasis, that too is usually part of the poet's design.

You should then discuss the sound of the passage, including in your discussion the quality and length of the sounds. Usually this discussion takes into consideration assonance, alliteration, consonance, onomatopoeia, and specially related patterns of consonant and vowel sounds.

Conclusion

Here you should evaluate the success of the passage. Did the prosody seem appropriate to the rhetorical situation? Did it conflict, and if so, does that conflict provide grounds for an adverse judgment? Did the prosody augment the idea of the passage? Did it give the passage more power than the idea alone would do? In short, answer the question of how well the sounds and the rhythms succeeded in being an instrument of communication and a device by which the poet may evoke the proper emotions in the reader.

HINTS

1. At the beginning of your paper you should provide a triple-spaced version of the passage under analysis. Make at least two carbon copies in order to employ them for various analytical purposes, as in the sample following, where one copy shows metrics, and the others show alliteration and assonance.

2. Number each line in your example, beginning with *1*, regardless of the length of the passage.

3. Indicate the separate feet by a diagonal line (/). Indicate caesurae by a double diagonal (//). If you wish to make refinements, reserve the double diagonal for caesurae which do not affect the pitch of the voice; use a triple diagonal (///) for voice-lowering caesurae and a reverse double diagonal (\\) for voice-raising caesurae.

4. Indicate lightly stressed syllables by the circle (o), or, if your instructor prefers, by the half circle (ᴗ) or cross (x). Show heavily stressed syllables by the acute accent or slash (′ or /) and by the grave accent (\).

5. Circle letters indicating a pattern of alliteration and assonance, and draw lines indicating the connection. Different colored pencils are effective in distinguishing the various patterns, or, if you use only one pencil or pen, you might attach numbers to the phrases in order to distinguish the patterns. Any easily recognized system that is convenient for you is acceptable. It is also a good idea to circle the metrical variations (thus, anapaests and trochees might be circled to help you identify them easily when you begin to write).

6. At the bottom of your pages, provide a key to your circles and lines.

7. It is best to use a standard pronunciation guide for your discussion of sounds. You may employ one of the standard collegiate dictionaries. If you have had formal linguistic study, use the phonemic or phonetic systems; otherwise you will probably find the dictionary system more convenient.

8. Underline all sounds to which you are calling attention. If you refer to a sound within a word (e.g., the *l* sound in *calling*), underline only that sound.

9. If you prepare these versions with care, half your job is over. All you need do after this preparation is to describe what you have analyzed and noted. Here your connecting lines of the same types or colors can help you immeasurably, for the lines and colors are obvious and will help you remember important variations and devices of sound.

Sample Theme

A Prosodic Analysis of Lines 232–243 of Tennyson's "Morte D'Arthur" [4]

Metrical Variation

```
  o    o  /    o   /    o   /     o  \    o  \
But the o- / ther swift- / ly strode // from ridge / to ridge, //      1
    ─1──

  /    o    o   /   o   /    o   \    o   /
Clothed with / his breath, // and look- / ing, // as / he walk'd, //    2
 ──4──  ──────1──────      ──────2──        ──1──
```

---

4 *The Complete Poetical Works of Tennyson*, W. J. Rolfe, ed. (Cambridge, Mass.: Houghton Mifflin Co., 1898), p. 66. All quotations from "Morte D'Arthur" are taken from this page.

Lar-ger / than hu- / man // on / the fro- / zen hills. ///   3
—6——   ——2——   —1—

He heard / the deep / be-hind / him, // and / a cry   4
                              —2—   —1—

Be-fore. /// His own / thought drove / him // like / a goad. ///   5
                      ——3——   —4—   —1—

Dry clash'd / his har- / ness // in / the i- / cy caves   6
——3——   ——2——   —1—

And bar-   ren/chasms, // and all / to left / and right   7
——2——   ——6——

The bare / black cliff / clang'd round / him, // as / he based   8
        ——3——   ——3——   —4—   —1—

His feet / on juts / of slip- / pe-ry crag // that rang   9
                                      —1—

Sharp- smit- / ten // with / the dint / of ar- / med heels— ///   10
——3——   —4—   —1—

And on / a sud- / den, // lo! // the lev- / el lake, //   11
        ——2——   —4—

And the / long glor- / ies // of / the win- / ter moon. ///   12
—5——   ——3——   —4—   —1—

1 = Anapaest, or effect of anapaest.   4 = Effect of imperfect feet.

2 = Amphibrach, or the effect   5 = Pyrrhic.
    of amphibrach.
                                           6 = Trochee, or the
3 = Spondee.   effect of trochee.

Alliteration

But the other swiftly strode from ridge to ridge   1

Clothed with his breath, and looking, as he walk'd,   2

Larger than human on the frozen hills.   3

He heard the deep behind him, and a cry   4

Before. His own thought drove him like a goad.   5

Dry clash'd his harness in the icy caves   6

And barren chasms, and all to left and right   7

The bare black cliff clang'd round him, as he based   8

His feet on juts of slippery crag that rang   9

Sharp-smitten with the dint of armed heels —   10

And on a sudden, lo! the level lake,   11

And the long glories of the winter moon.   12

$\cdots\cdots\cdots = S$

$\text{— — —} = H \text{ aspirate}$

$\text{—·—} = K$

$\text{———} = B$

$\cdots\cdots\cdots = L$

Assonance

But the other swiftly strode from ridge to ridge,   1

Clothed with his breath, and looking, as he walk'd,   2

Larger than human on the frozen hills,   3

He heard the deep behind him, and a cry   4

Before. His own thought drove him like a goad.   5

Dry clash'd his harness in the icy caves   6

And barren chasms, and all to left and right   7

The bare black cliff clang'd round him, as he based   8

His feet on juts of slippery crag that rang   9

Sharp-smitten with the dint of armed heels —   10

And on a sudden, lo! the level lake,   11

And the long glories of the winter moon.   12

$$= \bar{O}$$

$$= \bar{I}$$

$$= \breve{A}$$

$$= \ddot{A}$$

The poem itself is a dramatic tale within a tale. The poet Hall tells the story; the narrator, Tennyson's speaker, who relates what Hall tells, has been dozing before the story, while the parson sleeps all through the telling. Slightly comic as it is, this sleep also lends a dream-like quality to the poem and enables Tennyson to achieve his "high" purpose. For the poem is about the passing of the old order (symbolized by the death of Arthur), and the old order does not pass without the regret of those who are left behind, who magnify and elevate the order to unparalleled heights. Tennyson's technique of removing the story from his own voice to Hall's makes this elevation possible, and actually justifies the claim that the story is a "Homeric" echo. In short, the poem captures the magic of the old order, and also its heroic, brave, undaunted ruggedness.

The passage I have selected for prosodic analysis moves in sympathy with this passing of the heroic age. The motion described is from the mountainous heights where Arthur was wounded to the level lake on which he will travel to his final rest—from the elevated to the low. It is reasonable to expect, therefore, that the passage should convey the impression of Sir Bedivere's exertion as he performs his last service for his dying monarch. The passage should be strong just as Bedivere is strong; it should uncompromisingly support the elevated and magical evocation of the poem itself; it should end on an emotional key similar to that experienced by Bedivere as he reaches his goal. My study of the passage will attempt to show the degree of Tennyson's success in achieving these aims.

The rhythm of the passage is everywhere alive to the dramatic situation I have described. The basic metrical pattern is iambic pentameter, but this pattern is highly varied. Any description of Tennyson's metrical variations is arbitrary, but with this reservation I will try to describe them.

The passage opens with an anapaest (But the o-), and there is another anapaest in line 9. Tennyson seems to like anapaests, for he creates their effect in many other lines by inserting a pause within an iamb, and then making the heavy stress of the iamb fall onto a preposition or a conjunction which must then fit into the next iamb (which usually contains the object of the preposition), as follows:

$$\overset{\circ}{} \quad \overset{/}{} \quad \overset{\circ}{} \quad \overset{\circ}{} \quad \overset{\circ}{} \quad \overset{/}{}$$
and looking // as he walked

$$\overset{\circ}{\text{than}} \overset{/}{\text{hu}}\overset{\circ}{\text{man}} \; // \; \overset{\circ}{\text{on}} \overset{\circ}{\text{the}} \overset{/}{\text{frozen}} \text{ hills}$$

$$\overset{\circ}{\text{be}}\overset{/}{\text{hind}} \overset{\circ}{\text{him}} \; // \; \overset{\circ}{\text{and}} \overset{\circ}{\text{a}} \overset{/}{\text{cry}}$$

He creates this type of apparent anapaestic variation in lines 2 (twice), 4, 5, 6, 8, 10, and 12. A related variation is the frequent appearance of an amphibrachic rhythm, which is produced in lines 2, 3, 4, 6, 7, and 11. In line 11, for example, the first five syllables precede the caesura:

$$\overset{\circ}{\text{And}} \overset{\backslash}{\text{on}} / \overset{\circ}{\text{a}} \overset{\backslash}{\text{sud-}} / \overset{\circ}{\text{den,}} \; // \; \overset{/}{\text{lo!}} \; // \; \cdots$$

Because *And on* seems to form a foot, *a sudden* seems to be a unit too, since there is no other syllable to go with *sudden*. Thereby an apparent amphibrachic rhythm is formed. Still another related variation is that of the apparently imperfect feet in lines 2, 5, 8, 10, 11, and 12. These imperfect feet are usually produced by their closeness to a caesura, as in the following:

$$\overset{\circ}{\text{The}} \overset{/}{\text{bare}} / \text{ black cliff} / \text{ clang'd round} / \overset{\circ}{\text{him}} \; //$$

$$\overset{\backslash}{\text{as}} / \overset{\circ}{\text{he}} \overset{/}{\text{based}} \cdots$$

In this line *him* is in effect all by itself, though in theory it is the unstressed syllable in the iamb $\overset{\circ}{him} // \overset{\backslash}{as}$. But a theoretical foot does not an actual make, and I submit that the two words do not belong together.

Perhaps the most effective metrical variation in the passage is the frequent use of spondees, which appear in lines 5, 6, 8 (twice), 10, and 12. These substitutions, occurring mainly in the section where Sir Bedivere is forcing his way down the frozen hills, permit the lines to ring out, as in:

$$\overset{\circ}{\text{The}} \overset{/}{\text{bare}} / \text{ black cliff} / \text{ clang'd round} /$$

and

$$\text{Dry clash'd} / \overset{\circ}{\text{his}} \overset{/}{\text{har}}\overset{\circ}{\text{ness}} \cdots$$

Other, less significant, substitutions are the trochees in lines 3 and 7, and the pyrrhic in line 12. The total effect of these variations is to support the grand, free conception of the heroic action described in the lines.

Many of the variations I have described are produced by Tennyson's free handling of his sentence structure, which results in a free placement of the caesurae and in a free use of end-stopping and enjambment. It is interesting to note that four of the first five lines are end-stopped (two by commas, two by periods). Bedivere is walking, but exerting himself during these lines, and apparently can be making short rests to gather strength for his ordeal. The ordeal comes during the next four lines, when he makes his precarious descent; none of the lines containing this description is end-stopped. Bedivere is disturbed (being goaded by "his own thought"), but he must keep going, and we may presume that the free sentence structure and the free metrical variation enforce the difficulty and mental disturbance he is experiencing. But in the last two lines, when he has reached the lake and therefore his goal, the lines "relax" with feminine caesurae exactly following the fifth syllables. In other words, the sentence structure of the last two lines is fairly regular, an effect designed perhaps to indicate the return to order and beauty after the previous, rugged chaos.

This rhythmical virtuosity is accompanied by a similar brilliance of sound. Alliteration is an obvious and startling device in these lines; some notable examples are the recurrent aspirate *h*'s in lines 3–6 (*h*uman, *h*e, *h*eard, be*h*ind, *h*im, *h*is, *h*arness), the *b*'s in lines 7 and 8 (*b*arren, *b*are, *b*lack), the *s*'s in line 1 (*s*wiftly *s*trode), the *k*'s in lines 6–9 (*c*lash'd, *c*aves, *c*hasms, *c*liff, *c*lang'd, *c*rag), and the *l*'s in lines 11 and 12 (*l*o, *l*evel, *l*ake, *l*ong, g*l*ories). Assonance is also working throughout as a unifying device, as in the $\bar{o}$ pattern of lines 1, 2, 3, and 5 (str*o*de, cl*o*thed, fr*o*zen, *o*wn, dr*o*ve, g*oa*d), the $\breve{a}$ pattern of lines 7, 8, and 9 (ch*a*sms, cl*a*ng'd, bl*a*ck, cr*a*g, r*a*ng), the $\ddot{a}$ pattern of line 10 (sh*a*rp, *a*rmed), the $\bar{\imath}$ pattern of lines 4–7 (l*i*ke, dr*y*, *i*cy, r*i*ght). One might also remark that there are many high-front vowel sounds (i.e., $\bar{e}, \bar{a}, \bar{\imath}, \breve{a}$) in the first ten lines. But in the last two lines, which describe the level lake and the moon, Tennyson introduces a number of low, back vowels (i.e., $\breve{o}, \breve{u}, \bar{o}, \breve{o}, \tilde{o}, \breve{u}, \overline{oo}$). The striking effect of the vowels in these last two lines can be pointed out only when they are heard immediately after the two preceding lines:

> . . . as he based
> His feet on juts of slippery crag that rang
> Sharp-smitten with the dint of armed heels—
> And on a sudden, lo! the level lake,
> And the long glories of the winter moon.
>
> —lines 8–12

As these last two lines are read, their back, low vowels make possible a lowering of vocal pitch and a certain relaxation of vocal tension, and thereby they are eminently appropriate at this point in the poem, when Sir Bedivere has attained his goal.

The last two lines are, in fact, almost totally onomatopoeic, since the liquid *l* sounds are definitely imitative of the gentle lapping of lake waves upon a shore and in the line of the moon. There are other examples of onomatopoeia in this short passage, too. In line 2 Tennyson brings out the detail of Sir Bedivere's walking in the presumably

cold air "Clothed with his breath," and in the following five lines
Tennyson employs many words with the aspirate *h* (e.g., *h*is *h*arness);
in this context, these sounds suggest Sir Bedivere's labored breath as
he carries his royal burden. Similarly, the explosive stops *b* and *k*, *d*
and *t* in lines 6–10 seem to be imitative of the sounds of Sir Bedivere's
feet as he places them on the "juts of slippery crag."

This short passage, therefore, is a mine of prosodic skill—a virtuoso
piece that I do not expect to find on every page I shall read of English
poetry. The sounds and the rhythms of the words and lines themselves,
put into this context by Tennyson, actually speak along with the meaning; they emphasize the grandeur of Arthur and his faithful follower,
and for one brief moment bring out the magic that Tennyson associated with the fading past. In the poem, the outright glory of this passage makes understandable Sir Bedivere's previous reluctance to cast
away King Arthur's sword. Such glory is not to be thrown away easily;
but now it is gone, and we can regain it only in our imaginations, or in
Tennyson's poem.

14

The Theme Analyzing the Style
in a Short Section of Prose

S TYLE is usually understood to mean the way in which a writer employs his words, phrases, and sentences to achieve his desired effects. It should be distinguished from *structure*, which is concerned with organization and arrangement of the work as a whole. Though *style* may be used loosely to comprise the writer's entire craft, for this theme you will be concerned with the word in its narrower sense. As you read a work of literature you become aware of its style, even though you may not be able to describe the style accurately after you have finished reading. The main obstacle to discussing style is that you do not have the descriptive vocabulary for embodying your perceptions, and so the best you can say is that the style is simply "good," "bad," "crisp," "elegant," "formal," "brilliant," or the like, with an uneasy hope that no one will ask what you mean. Perhaps your previous experience with literature and with composition has been concerned not so much with style as with content. The result is that analyzing style is like experiencing weightlessness for the first time.

Let us grant, then, that style is difficult to describe and analyze. You may have discovered, however, that critics and reviewers in the Sunday papers and elsewhere are constantly praising or condemning writers for their styles. You can see the desirability of being familiar with an approach to style, for how else can you formulate your own opinions? What do the critics look for? What does your instructor look for? What are their standards for a style? What criteria do they use as a basis of judgment? Is it possible, in short, for a student to be let in on the "mysteries" of discussing style, or should these arcane matters remain in the hands of the critics, forever out of reach?

PURPOSE OF STYLISTIC ANALYSIS

The object of your theme is to make you aware of style: what it is, how to discuss it, how to evaluate it, how to relate it to the achievement of the literary work as a whole, how to define the characteristics of each writer's style. Because style is concerned with diction, phrases, sentences, and sound and rhythm—together with the relationship of all these matters to the entire work under consideration—you will have to wrestle with sentences and words, and from time to time may be thrown on your ear. But if you persist you will develop the ability to make some accurate and useful observations about a writer's style. You will learn much, and will be well on the way toward a dependable means of evaluating literature.

LIMITATIONS

In your analysis you will not be able to make observations about an entire work because of limited space. To write this assignment, you need only to take a short passage—a single paragraph is best, although a passage of dialogue is also satisfactory—and use it as the basis of your observations. As with the prosodic analysis, it is usually best to select a well-written passage or else one that conveys a good deal of the writer's argument, for the author will have devoted his best skill and energy to such passages. You must be aware of the limitations in this selection, for the discussion of one paragraph does not necessarily apply to the whole work in which the paragraph appears. But if you make these points—that your method of analysis would be the same for any passage in the whole book, and that the paragraph is important in the book—the generalizations you make will have implications for the entire work. The authenticity of your remarks will depend upon the skill and knowledge you show in your analysis. Always beware, however, of making hasty generalizations. With these reservations, your theme about style will be of great value to you.

MAIN PROBLEM

The main problem you will encounter in this assignment is how to discover your writer's style. Suppose, for example, you choose to analyze a piece of dramatic prose, or a passage of dialogue from a novel. Or suppose you select a passage from a novel that is told from the first-person point of view. When you speak about the style of these passages, are you describing the *writer's* style or the *speaker's* style? Suppose that you analyze, in the same work, two passages that are dissimilar in style? Did the writer's style change, or did he adapt it to fit the different places or speakers? And if he did so adapt it, what are you trying to discover by an analysis of style?

The answer seems obvious. In your analysis you are trying to determine the degree of the writer's *control* over his subject matter. Control is what matters. If you discover that your writer adheres to the same style throughout his work, that fact might lead you to conclude that he has inadequate control over his subject matter. But you should ask some further questions: does he have some definite end in view in using this one style? If so, what is it? Is he successful? The aim of your analysis is always to describe specific characteristics and to make at least partial judgments of why these characteristics appear and what they contribute to the work.

To see how this aim might be fulfilled, look at the following example, from *The Merchant of Venice*, Act I, Scene ii:

> If to do were as easy as to know what were good to do, chapels had been churches and poor men's cottages princes' palaces. It is a good divine that follows his own instructions: I can easier teach twenty what were good to be done, than to be one of the twenty to follow mine own teaching. . . .

From the style of this passage, it seems clear that Portia (the speaker) is a woman with a rapid mind, well befitting her masquerade as an intelligent lawyer-judge later in the play. Her first sentence uses simple diction in a complex structure. Of her first fourteen words, six compose infinitives, and two are verbs; a total of eight words out of fourteen, or over 55 per cent, therefore serve as verbs or verbals. Her mind, in other words, is active. The first fourteen words are also part of an if-clause, dependent upon the verb in the following main clause. The ability to use subordination in sentences is regarded as the mark of a good mind and a good style. Portia, too, shows an ability to use rhetoric—in this sentence the rhetorical device called *zeugma* (the use of a single word with double grammatical weight).[1] The main clause of the first sentence is equivalent to two clauses, but the verb is used only once: "chapels had been churches and poor men's cottages [had been] princes' palaces." Portia's language is exceedingly simple, in other words, but she shows a fine sense of rhetorical and logical balance.

To be contrasted with Portia's speech is this one by Ophelia in *Hamlet*, Act IV, Scene v:

> Well, God 'ild you! They say, the owl was a baker's daughter. Lord! we know what we are, but know not what we may be. God be at your table!

Ophelia makes this speech after she has become insane. Her words are simple, and her sentences are disconnected. Just when there seems to be a relationship among them (between sentences two and three) her thought is swiftly broken, and her last sentence seems as random as her first. Had Shakespeare introduced the intellectual toughness of Portia's speech here, he would not have shown a broken mind but an alert one in all its powers.

---

[1] This definition pertains to zeugma in its simplest sense. When a word works doubly grammatically, however, it frequently takes on two meanings, so that many people regard the double meaning as essential to a definition of zeugma. Thus, in Pope's line "Or stain her honor, or her new brocade," *stain* carries double weight grammatically, and also double meaning, first as a metaphoric stain upon honor, and second as a literal stain upon a brocade. In this line, therefore, *stain* works as a zeugma, a metaphor, and a pun. Complications like these are not unusual, but are not essential.

Thus he gave Ophelia these disconnected sentences, so unlike her coherent speeches in poetry earlier in the play.

The point about these two passages is that, though they differ in style, Shakespeare's control and artistry do not. In fact, the passages show his mastery of dramatic prose. The study of style should aim toward a description of the writer's ability to control his words to serve his needs.

APPROACHES TO STYLE

The three chief ways to describe style are (a) the analysis of the grammar in a passage, (b) the analysis of the rhythm and sound, and (c) the analysis of the words, their denotation and connotation, their influences upon each other in context, their symbolic values, their functions in similes, metaphors, and other rhetorical figures.

Analysis of Grammar

Though commonly avoided, the nomenclature of grammar is a useful tool in describing a writer's sentences. As you have been taught grammar, you should not have trouble undertaking the analysis of grammar in your passage. For example, the following sentences from the beginning of Hemingway's *Farewell to Arms* have been justly praised by critics:

> (1) In the late summer of that year we lived in a house in a village that looked across the river and the plain to the mountains. (2) In the bed of the river there were pebbles and boulders, dry and white in the sun, and the water was clear and swiftly moving and blue in the channels. (3) Troops went by the house and down the road and the dust they raised powdered the leaves of the trees. (4) The trunks of the trees too were dusty and the leaves fell early that year and we saw the troops marching along the road and the dust rising and leaves, stirred by the breeze, falling and the soldiers marching and afterward the road bare and white except for the leaves.[2]

You will observe that in this paragraph Hemingway employs the word *and* many times. Of the four sentences, the last three are all compound sentences (independent clauses joined by *and*), whereas the first one is complex. Usually compound sentences do not demonstrate cause-and-effect or other relations and so are best used in narrative description. A number of compound sentences tend to declare, rather than to analyze (similarities between Hemingway's passage and parts of the King James Bible have been noticed in this connection). Also, compound sentences strung together may, under some circumstances, suggest resignation on the speaker's part. These remarks apply here.

---

2 (New York: Charles Scribner's Sons, 1929), p. 3.

In this passage there are also many prepositional phrases. There are six-teen phrases, to be exact (one with a compound object). Of these sixteen, twelve are adverbial, and of these twelve, eight modify verbs. This number is to be contrasted with the number of single-word adverbs—three. The proportion of phrases is so high that you might justifiably conclude that the characteristic method of modification in the passage is the use of phrases. Prepositional phrases usually require many *in*'s, *of*'s, and *the*'s; so a passage with many phrases would likely contain many monosyllabic words. In this passage, there are 126 words; 103 have one syllable; twenty-two have two syllables; and one has three syllables. The method of modifi-cation thus has a close relationship to the simple, rather stark diction of the passage, for if Hemingway had relied upon single-word adverbs he would necessarily have used more polysyllabic words. (Notice that the three single-word adverbs are all polysyllabic: *swiftly, early, afterward.* The longest word in the passage is an adverb.)

You can see that a knowledge of grammatical terms (in this example, a knowledge of conjunction, compound sentences, complex sentences, ad-verbs, phrases, nouns) aids in the analysis, description, and evaluation of style. Without this knowledge you are handicapped in discussing style.

Let us take a sentence from another writer. The following is from Theodore Dreiser's *The Titan*. It has probably never been praised by anyone:

> From New York, Vermont, New Hampshire, Maine had come a strange company, earnest, patient, determined, unschooled in even the primer of refinement, hungry for something the significance of which, when they had it, they could not even guess, anxious to be called great, determined so to be without ever knowing how.[3]

This sentence begins with a prepositional phrase used adverbially, with four objects of the preposition. Then Dreiser introduces the verb (*had come*), and then the subject of the verb (*strange company*). Immediately after the subject there are three adjectives which modify it. There is then a fourth adjective (*unschooled*) modified by an adverb phrase (*in even the primer*), and the object of the preposition is modified by an adjective phrase (*of refinement*). Then there is a fifth adjective (*hungry*) modifying the subject of the sentence. This fifth adjective has complex modification; first there is an adverb phrase (*for something*), and then the noun *some-thing* is modified by an adjective clause which in turn has with it an adverb clause (*the significance of which, when they had it, they could not even guess*). The original series of adjectives is resumed with *anxious*, which is modified by the adverbial infinitive *to be called great*. The ad-jective series ends with the seventh, *determined*, which is modified by the

---

3 (New York: Dell Publishing Co., Inc. [Copyright World Publishing Co.] 1959), p. 25.

adverbial infinitive phrase *so to be,* which is modified by the adverbial *without ever knowing how.*

If you have been confused by this grammatical description, you will readily agree that the sentence begins simply but unusually and becomes difficult and involved. It is inverted and rhetorically dramatic; it depends for its full effect upon close study in its context on the printed page, whereas the example from Hemingway could be readily followed if someone read it aloud. In Dreiser's defense, you might say that the sentence explores a difficult avenue of thought: Dreiser is describing the makeup of a giant, a *titan,* and theoretically his language should therefore be grand and sweeping. In fact, this sentence fits into his design, for its seven adjectives build up to a cumulative impression of bigness. In its way, this sentence is quite effective.

Among other things, grammatical analysis reveals the complexity or simplicity of a writer's style. You should observe whether the sentences fall into patterns. Are most of the sentences simple, compound, or complex? Why? Is there a recurrence of any rhetorical devices that can be described grammatically (e.g., parallelism, zeugma, chiasmus)? Are the sentences mainly *loose* or *periodic,* and why? Always be alert to the special characteristics of your passage. For example, you might notice that its sentences are filled with many adjectives, or with subordinate clauses. Your grammatical study should conclude by trying to answer the question of why the elements are as they are. In this way you will see the usefulness of analyzing grammar when you discuss style, for the two are inseparably identified.

A word of caution is perhaps needed. The description of grammar can become deadly and sterile if it leads to no generalizations. It is not an end in itself. But the labor of grammatical analysis can produce stimulating and sometimes startling results.

Rhythm and Sound

RHYTHM   Some analysts of style become vague or rapturous when they speak about the rhythm of prose. The reason is not far to seek, for prose rhythm is difficult to analyze and still more difficult to describe. If you keep your ear alert, however, and if you combine the results of your hearing with the analysis of grammar in a passage, you can arrive at accurate and useful generalizations about prose rhythms. The rhythm of prose can seldom be accurately described by iambs, trochees, dactyls, and so on, for words which could be measured neatly by feet in poetry are actually parts of some larger rhythmic pattern in prose. The rhythm of prose, in short, is generally vaster than that of poetry, in keeping with the prose writer's general intention to develop his thoughts extensively. To feel the quality of prose rhythm, read this passage:

. . . But when a Man's Fancy gets *astride* on his Reason, when Imagination is at Cuffs with the Senses, and common Understanding, as well as common Sense, is Kickt out of Doors; the first Proselyte he makes, is Himself, and when that is once compass'd, the Difficulty is not so great in bringing over others; A strong Delusion always operating from *without*, as vigorously as from *within*. For, Cant and Vision are to the Ear and the Eye, the same that Tickling is to the Touch. Those Entertainments and Pleasures we most value in Life, are such as *Dupe* and play the Wag with the Senses. For, if we take an Examination of what is generally understood by *Happiness*, as it has Respect, either to the Understanding or the Senses, we shall find all its Properties and Adjuncts will herd under this short Definition: That, *it is a perpetual Possession of being well Deceived.*[4]

Though these sentences could easily be scanned as iambs and anapaests, you will notice that it is more accurate to submerge many of the accents in the bigger, more important rhythmical pattern; i.e.,

But when a Man's Fancy gets *astride* on his Reason,

when Imagination is at Cuffs with the Senses . . .

You will immediately see that there is rhythm here, but that stresses are placed upon fewer syllables than in a verse passage of comparable length. Notice, in fact, that in prose the individual cadence groups, or phraseological groups, are the basic units, and that the cadence groups are fitted into the separate parts making up the sentence. The groups can be analyzed with the help of the punctuation marks and the natural though slight pauses between subjects and predicates, compound subjects, etc. Thus the first sentence might be laid out as follows:

But when a Man's Fancy	gets *astride* on his Reason,
when Imagination	is at Cuffs with the Senses,
and common Understanding,	
as well as common Sense,	
	is Kickt out of Doors;
the first Proselyte he makes,	
	is Himself,
and when that is once compass'd,	
the Difficulty is not so great	in bringing over others;
A strong Delusion always operating	from *without*,
as vigorously	
	as from *within*.

----

4 Jonathan Swift, *A Tale of a Tub*, Second ed., A. C. Guthkelch and D. Nichol Smith, eds. (London: Oxford University Press, 1958), p. 171.

With this scheme may be contrasted a rhythmic analysis of the sentence from Dreiser:

From New York,
Vermont,
New Hampshire,
Maine
had come a strange company,

earnest,
patient,
determined,
unschooled in even the primer

of refinement,

hungry for something

the significance of which,
when they had it,
they could not even guess,

anxious to be called great,
determined so to be

without ever knowing how.

Though it is unwise to make extensive generalizations from only these two schematic patterns, you can easily see a difference between the two. The unit lengths of Swift's sentence are longer and more evenly balanced than those in the sentence by Dreiser, where the units begin thinly, but become longer. Your job in analyzing a prose passage is to make a similar attempt to discover and to characterize its rhythms. To assist yourself, you should read the passage aloud and listen for its rises and falls, its lengths of utterance. It is also good to have a fellow student read the passage aloud to you, so that you will be better able to observe its rhythms.

SOUND   Despite the differences between poetry and prose, the various "poetic" devices such as alliteration, assonance, and onomatopoeia may also be at work in prose. You should be alert for them. Look at the example from Hemingway again. If you listen, you will hear that Hemingway employs assonance (e.g., sentence 3: h*o*use, d*o*wn, p*o*wdered; sentence 2: m*o*ving, bl*ue*; sentences 3 and 4: l*ea*ves, br*ee*ze, w*e*, tr*ee*s). Or, in the first sentence of the selection from Swift's *Tale of a Tub*, there are many short *ĭ* and short *ă* sounds. In fact, there is an extremely high proportion of high and central vowels (about 80 per cent). Perhaps these sounds illustrate not only the thin and rarefied quality of the human madness the speaker is describing, but also the volatile, choleric qualities of his mind. The effect of this attention to sound is to make the reader conscious of prose that is not just run of the mill. Although the passages are prose, therefore, they are closely controlled and have many poetic characteristics. In commenting upon the passages, you should certainly establish their similarity to poetry, and should include this fact in your evaluation of the style.

Diction—Meaning of Words in Context

This phase of stylistic study is the one in which you will probably feel most at home, for you have always been aware of the problems of meaning. You should observe, however, that a study of diction does not simply rely upon dictionary definitions, but goes beyond the meanings of the words to a study of their relationships in context. Words rarely exist by themselves, but are in a context in which one word affects another, and your interest here should be to observe and record these relationships.

Look at the words in your passage and see where they take you. You are on an exploration, and may or may not discover something valuable. Some guidelines for your itinerary might be the following questions, which you should ask of your passage: Are any important words repeated? Why? Are there any unusual words? Surprising words? Why? Do the words have common etymologies? (E.g., are most of the words Anglo-Saxon in origin, or are there many of Latin or Greek derivation? Consult your dictionaries for etymologies.) Does the author use many adjectives before a noun? After a noun? Why? What is the effect? Are the words in the passage mainly specific or general? Concrete or abstract? Why? (Observe in the passage from Hemingway that the words are mainly specific and concrete, whereas in that from Dreiser there are many abstract words; what is the difference in effect caused by this difference in diction?) Are any of the words allusive; i.e., do they suggest other contexts, literary, historical, scientific, or whatever? What are the connotations of the words as distinguished from the denotations? Does the passage rely upon these connotations? How? Is there dialect in the passage? What is its effect? You can see that your understanding of point-of-view is relevant here, for the *persona* of the piece will create the nature of the diction (characterize as narrators: Huckleberry Finn, Holden Caulfield, Jane Eyre, or the speaker of "Only the Dead Know Brooklyn" by Thomas Wolfe).

These are the main questions you will attempt to answer in your analysis of diction, though there may be others that will come naturally out of the passage you select. Your principal tools here are a dictionary, your reading experience, and your alertness. Be on the lookout for relationships, but do not invent them if they do not exist. Be ready, however, to take the hints provided you by the author.

THE ORGANIZATION OF YOUR THEME

Your theme should have the following points. In the body you may arrange your analysis into any order you wish. Please recognize that though the theme is a general one on style, any one of the points in the body could easily be developed into an extensive theme in its own right.

Introduction

A brief description of the work from which you have selected the passage you will analyze, followed by a brief discussion of the purpose and intent of the passage you have selected, will suffice. Many of the questions you need to answer are in the opening section of the prosodic analysis. The main point to answer here, however, is "What is the relationship of my passage to the work as a whole? What was the passage trying to do, and how well did it succeed?"

Body

In this section you should consider three points.

1. A consideration of the grammar of your passage. You should also observe the lengths of the sentences, but try to make your count point toward worthwhile conclusions. By modern standards, an average sentence is about 25 words long. If you have five sentences of, say, a fifteen-word average, with lengths from five to twenty words, you may say that the sentences are short, terse, sparse, laconic, brief. If, on the other hand, the sentences average fifty words, you can say that they are full, round, rotund (or perhaps wordy or rambling).

2. The rhythm and sound of the passage. You may wish to integrate this discussion with your consideration of grammar and punctuation, as grammatical and phraseological units dictate rhythms. Perhaps you might be observing a long sentence characterized by many extensive rhythmical units, as in the following by Edmund Burke:

> I am convinced we have a degree of delight, and that no small one, in the real misfortunes and pains of others; for let the affection be what it will in appearance, if it does not make us shun such objects, if on the contrary it induces us to approach them, if it makes us dwell upon them, in this I conceive we must have a delight or pleasure of some species or other in contemplating objects of this kind.
>
> —*A Philosophical Enquiry Into The Origin Of Our Ideas Of The Sublime And Beautiful*, Section XIV

Or perhaps you are reading short sentences and rhythms, as in this passage from John Webster:

> Now you're brave fellows. Caesar's fortune was harder than Pompey's: Caesar died in the arms of prosperity, Pompey at the feet of disgrace.
>
> —*The Duchess of Malfi*, V, v, 57–61

Study your passage carefully and observe not only the rhythms but the sounds. The sample theme, analyzing a passage from Faulkner, points out instances of alliteration and assonance. If you study your passage carefully you should make worthwhile and interesting conclusions.

3. The diction. This section might well be the longest, for you are always aware of problems of meaning. Discuss the diction in context and try to make observations about its relationship to the thought and intent of the passage.

Conclusion

Make a concluding evaluation of the style—a summary of your findings. How well did the passage contribute to the entire work? If it did not contribute much, did it detract?

HINTS

1. This theme is designed to increase your perceptions, sensitivity, and appreciation. Listen carefully; read carefully; try to feel the full force of the passage you select.
2. Make a copy of your passage and place it at the start of your theme.
3. Number each sentence in your passage.
4. When you write, use quotations to illustrate your points. Do not just quote in a vacuum, however, but explain your point and make your analysis before or immediately after your quotation.
5. *Underline* all elements to which you wish to draw attention.
6. Always indicate the sentence numbers of your quotations.

Sample Theme

An Analysis of the Prose Style in the Last Paragraph of Chapter 20 in William Faulkner's *Light in August* [5]

(1) It is as though they had merely waited until he could find something to pant with, to be reaffirmed in triumph and desire with, with this last left of honor and pride and life. (2) He hears above his heart the thunder increase, myriad and drumming. (3) Like a long sighing of wind in trees it begins, then they sweep into sight, borne now upon a cloud of phantom dust. (4) They rush past, forwardleaning in the saddles, with brandished arms, beneath whipping ribbons from slanted and eager lances; with tumult

---

[5] From *Light in August*, by William Faulkner (New York: The Modern Library, 1950), pp. 431-32. Copyright 1932, and renewed 1959 by William Faulkner. Reprinted by permission of Random House, Inc.

and soundless yelling they sweep past like a tide whose crest is jagged with the wild heads of horses and the brandished arms of men like the crater of the world in explosion. (5) They rush past, are gone; the dust swirls skyward sucking, fades away into the night which has fully come. (6) Yet, leaning forward in the window, his bandaged head huge and without depth upon the twin blobs of his hands upon the ledge, it seems to him that he still hears them: the wild bugles and the clashing sabres and the dying thunder of hooves.

The passage I have selected is the concluding paragraph of the Joe Christmas–Gail Hightower story in Faulkner's *Light in August*. The paragraph, in the present tense, describes Hightower's dying thoughts, which are passing from consideration of the apotheosis of Joe Christmas to the galloping cavalry. This vision of the cavalry had earlier been Hightower's plague, but here it indicates his mental "triumph and desire." Previously vague and by some thought to be sacrilegious, the men and horses now illustrate Hightower's final vision of truth— namely, that all men are brothers and that human life at any moment is on a grand crest rushing toward a final, glorious shore. Just as Hightower's vision is affirmative and grand, so should Faulkner's style be affirmative and bold. It should illustrate the power of language, and my belief is that it does.

The grammar, for example, is carefully controlled. None of the six sentences is exactly like any of the others, although sentences 4 and 5 begin in the same way. The entire passage is framed by two complex sentences (1 and 6), and sentence 4 is a long compound-complex sentence. Sentence 2 is simple, and sentences 3 and 5 are compound (though neither of these compound sentences has a conjunction joining the two independent clauses). All the sentences show care, skill, and variety, plus a certain boldness. The first sentence, for example, is unusual and interesting. At the end of the adverb clause in this sentence Faulkner uses the word *with*, ordinarily a preposition, and then repeats it at the end of the infinitive phrase, as though to emphasize his boldness:

until he could find something to pant *with*, to be reaffirmed in triumph and desire *with*, . . .

Then he uses *with* again immediately, but now in its ordinary position as a preposition:

with this last left of honor and pride and life.

This usage gives the passage both weight and emphasis.

Another strong device in the paragraph is the use of single and parallel modifiers following the word they modify. Thus, we have

the thunder . . . , *myriad* and *drumming* . . .

When the galloping cavalry comes by,

> They rush past, (1) *forwardleaning in the saddles,* (2) *with brandished arms,* (3) *beneath whipping ribbons* . . . (sentence 4)

This pattern of "back" modifiers is one of the most characteristic in Faulkner, as is also another pattern (also shown in the quotation from sentence 4), that of grammatical units appearing in threes, frequently connected by the conjunction *and*, as in:

> honor and pride and life
> and
> the wild bugles and the clashing sabres and the dying thunder of hooves.

One might notice that in this paragraph, of six sentences, these two patterns of three occur at the beginning and the end, as though Faulkner were making a neatly balanced frame.

Balance and control, in fact, are also characteristic of the rhythms in the paragraph. The passage is full and the pauses are correctly and judiciously placed; the voice is therefore measured into fairly full but varied cadence groups. The fullest group is the second part of sentence 4. This segment is breathtaking, perfectly in keeping with the massive advance of the galloping cavalry. With the last pause of the voice falling after *past,* there are twenty-seven words that must be spoken without a significant pause—an extremely long and full rhythmical development giving an almost panoramic sweep of the cavalry:

> like a tide whose crest is jagged with the wild heads of horses and the brandished arms of men like the crater of the world in explosion.

To be contrasted with this long, broad rhythm is the almost abrupt rhythm in the next sentence:

> They rush past,
>   are gone;
>   the dust swirls skyward sucking,
>   fades away into the night
>   which has fully come.

Also, since Hightower feels that he is dying, it is interesting to note the many falling (i.e., dying) rhythms in the concluding words; that is: *wild bugles, dashing sabres, dying thunder.* But the passage concludes on an up-beat, a note of resurrection, well in keeping with the movement of apotheosis developed by Faulkner throughout the entire chapter:

> the dying thunder of hooves.

In accord with this almost poetic control over rhythm, the sounds of the passage have many poetic characteristics. Faulkner uses assonance and alliteration in almost every line. Assonance appears in the long $\bar{\imath}$ of f*i*nd, tr*i*umph, des*i*re, pr*i*de, l*i*fe (sentence 1); the short $\breve{u}$ in th*u*nder, dr*u*mming, r*u*st, d*u*st, s*u*cking, come (2 and 5); the *ou* diphthong in n*ow*, and cl*ou*d (3); and the short $\breve{a}$ in s*a*ddles, br*a*ndished, and sl*a*nted (4). Alliteration appears in *l*ast *l*eft (1); *h*ears, *h*eart, *h*eard, *h*uge, *h*ands, *h*ears (2 and 6); and *s*ighing, *s*weep, *s*ight, *s*wirls, *s*kyward, *s*ucking (3 and 5). These patterns cannot be overlooked, and coming as they do in this climactic paragraph, they greatly emphasize the grand, "poetic" vision of the expiring Hightower.

The mastery already described is also apparent in the diction, which leads from mainly abstract words in the first two sentences to mainly concrete words in the last four. Yet amid the concreteness of Hightower's vision of the cavalry, Faulkner puts words which stress its abstractness. The dust is *phantom dust,* and the yelling of the cavalrymen is *soundless.* In addition, the parallel verbs describing the movement of the horses are rather muffled, and for this reason permit the suggestion that they are phantom-like to work:

> they *sweep* into sight (3)
> They *rush* past (4)
> they *sweep* past (4)
> They *rush* past (5)
>   *are gone* (5).

The greatest virtue of Faulkner's diction in the paragraph is its active, bold vividness, however. The language is virtually fearless in these phrases:

> the crater of the world in explosion (4)
> this last left of honor and pride and life (1)
> the dust swirls skyward sucking (5)
> forwardleaning in the saddles (4)

It takes bold, original thinking, and much confidence, to use language in this way. All the phrases are new, accurate, and fresh. Other phrases are remarkably vivid. My favorites are:

> the dying thunder of hooves (6)
> beneath whipping ribbons from slanted and eager
>   lances (4).

It takes something great to think of *eager* lances. But my comments are superfluous here.

All in all, this paragraph gleams out of the page. When I first read it through for this theme I perhaps *sensed* this quality, but after having analyzed the grammar, rhythm, sound, and diction I am amazed at how well the paragraph wears. Each time I reread it, I recognize more and more of the real scope of a master prose stylist, and Faulkner is that. The paragraph is alive, quick. It is a fitting and brilliant conclusion to the Joe Christmas strand of *Light in August*.

15

The Theme of Evaluation

$\mathcal{T}$HE ULTIMATE goal of all literary study is evaluation. Evaluation is closely allied with *judgment,* which is the faculty by which we can distinguish between good and bad, right and wrong, plausibility and implausibility, and so on. *Evaluation,* as used here, means the act of deciding what is good, bad, or mediocre. It requires a steady pursuit of the best—to be satisfied with less is to deny the best efforts of our greatest writers. Evaluation implies that there are ideal standards of excellence by which decisions about quality can be made, but it must be remembered that these standards are flexible in their application, and may be applicable to works of literature written in all places and ages.

Although evaluation is the goal of literary study, description is the means by which the goal is reached. Without evaluation and appreciation, however, the description of idea, form, and style is really beside the point; it becomes a peripheral issue, a vacuum. Too often a good student will avoid making any judgments or commitments at all, though he may beautifully describe, say, the prosody of a poem. Quite frequently, too, he feels comfortable as he goes about his discussion, because description, in contrast with evaluation, is "safe"; it does not require him to "go out on a limb." Evaluation frequently requires taking a debatable position, from which others might chop him down. No one likes to be exposed, even by someone else's assertion that an equally valid alternative exists.

Despite the obvious dangers and difficulties of evaluation, however, you must take positions on the works you read. Not to do so is to avoid the most vital pattern in your educational development. You yourself must learn to decide what is good, and not always rely upon your instructor to tell you. If you lose yourself in pure description, or if you merely take the safe way by following someone else's judgment, you are not doing the best for yourself. You need to develop your intellectual courage. Certainly during much of your career as a student you can get by with the simple statement, "This work is a great one," because most of the works you read are literary classics. But the perfunctory comment "This is great" is not enough, for you should always try to discover just what are the grounds for judgment. Your study of the classics, in other words, should be more than perfunctory. You should always attempt to learn what is good in good works, so that you will have grounds for evaluating and appreciating works that are not yet accepted as classics—recent works, or works by relatively unknown authors, or lesser works by well-known authors. Remember, you will not always be taking literature classes, and when you are on your own you will want to know how to judge for yourself.

You may sometimes find that works commonly adjudged to be good do not seem good to you. If such is the case, try to live with the work for a time. If you have ever played in a band or orchestra, or sung in a chorus, you surely have found some musical compositions distasteful when you first read them through. But, as you reapproached the composition day after day, and worked on it and learned it, you probably discovered that the work grew on you, and that you finally became convinced of its value. This process confirms the statement that you will learn to understand and to like a good work of art when you have the opportunity to do so. If, however, you find that despite prolonged exposure to the work, you still do not concur in the general favorable judgment, be as certain as you can that your reaction is based on rational and logically defensible grounds.

You should realize too that your ability to judge will be increased as you learn about more and more fine works. You must read as much and learn as much as you can, for in this way you will be establishing the qualities of good literature firmly in your mind, and, naturally, as these qualities become clearer to you, you will be able to evaluate with greater ease. Now, though, you have the task of evaluating a single work for your theme. This single assignment should have a definite bearing upon your judgment in future years, because careful effort now will permanently improve your critical faculties. Your instructor does not expect you to judge like a great critic, but he does expect that you bring to bear on your work all the ideas about good literature that you have acquired.

THE RATIONALE OF EVALUATION

There is no precise answer to the problem of how to justify an evaluation, and you would be misled if you were told that there is. Consequently evaluation is the most abstract, philosophical, and difficult writing you will do about literature, just as it is the most necessary. We must recognize that standards of taste, social mores, and even morals differ from society to society and age to age; nonetheless, some works of art have been adjudged good or even great by generation after generation, whereas others have been consigned to that vast dustbin "of historical interest only." The student therefore asks, "By what standards may a work be judged a good or great work?" and, "How do I make this judgment by myself?"

THE TASK OF EVALUATION

In your theme you must ask: "Is the work I have read good, fair, or bad?" or, "Is it beautiful or not?" You must answer this question on artistic, not ideological grounds. In other words, you might say that a political speech does a good job of rousing the populace to vote a certain way, and as a result that it is a good—and here you probably mean *effective*—speech. But in claiming that it is a great work of art you would have to judge it on artistic grounds, not on political ones; you would in addition have to determine whether it was important not only for the moment, but for all moments. As very few speeches rise above their time, most speeches are not great works of art.

In admiring a work, then, you must consider whether you have been misled by an excellence that is really minor. An atrocious piece of literature might have a superb control over form, for example, and you might therefore suppose it to be good. But if other considerations caused you to withhold your total assent from the work, this supposition would be foolish. In short, you must consider everything about the work you evaluate and not be diverted from your object by surface beauties.

THE STANDARDS FOR EVALUATION

There are many standards to help you evaluate a literary work. Some of the major ones are described below, and many have been suggested in earlier chapters. The terms involved are used and defined here in the senses to which they are usually restricted by people talking about literature. To the philosopher, the aesthetician, the student of semantics, the words are probably charged with other meanings, and a treatment of those meanings would necessitate a whole philosophical treatise. It should be emphasized, however, that one cannot think intelligently or seriously about literature without using these terms, and it is to help you interpret these words as they are generally used in regard to literature that they are included here.

Truth

Although *truth* or *truthful* is used in speaking of literature to mean *realism* or *realistic* (e.g., does Flaubert give a truthful picture of Emma Bovary's society?), its meaning here is restricted carefully. To speak of the truth is to imply generality and universality. Let us take a concrete illustration.

Sophocles' *Antigone* is a play which has survived the passage of 2400 years. It concerns a society (the Greek city-state with a ruling monarch) which no longer exists; it deals with a religious belief (that the souls of the unburied dead never find rest) which passed from currency centuries ago; it involves an idea (of a curse following an entire family) accepted now only by the least educated members of our society. Wherein, then, lies the appeal, the truth, of *Antigone,* which makes it as much alive for our age as it was for the Greeks of more than 2000 years ago?

The answer is at least partly in the permanence of the human problem that Antigone faces: "How do I reconcile my duty to obey the state with my duty to obey my conscience? And if the two conflict, which do I follow?" This dilemma, and the suffering which is inevitable to any man caught in it, regardless of which choice he makes, is one which men have probably faced since the beginning of time; while men and states exist, this conflict between laws and conscience will endure—and so will the great statement of that problem given in *Antigone*. In short, the play embodies, lives in terms of, and comments upon, one of the great *truths* of human life. It measures up, then, to one standard we use in deciding whether a work of art is good or bad, great or mediocre. But other criteria must also be considered.

The Joint Force and Full Result of All

This quotation is from Pope's *Essay on Criticism,* where most of what can be said about evaluation is said. Pope insisted that a critic should not judge a work simply by its parts, but should judge the *whole,* the entirety of the work. You can profit from Pope's wisdom. You should carefully consider the total effect of the work, both as an artistic form and as a cause of impressions and emotions in yourself. Your total impression is important. James Joyce used the concepts "whatness" and "radiance" in describing the totality of a work; that is, when a work seems to be entirely itself, the force of its totality impresses the reader in a moment of revelation, or radiance. Though this sort of experience is almost mystical, and consequently impossible to describe, you must search your reactions after reading a work and see if you have been impressed with a sense of totality. Bear in mind that a great work may be imperfect —there may be flaws in style and organization; characters may be imperfectly drawn—but if the sum total of the work is impressive, the flaws assume minor importance. In other words, even if the author can be attacked on technical matters, the total effect of his work may overshadow the adverse criticism. Thomas Hardy and Theodore Dreiser are two authors in point; their language can frequently be shown to be at fault. But a reading of their best works reveals them as superior novelists.

You should see, then, that one cannot judge a work as good or bad by reference to only one element within it. An interesting plot, a carefully handled structure, a touching love story, a valid moral—none of these attributes alone can justify a total judgment of "good." One can say, for example, that Dickens' *Oliver Twist* has an extremely ingenious plot, and that it arouses our emotions effectively. But to evaluate the novel fully one must take into consideration several questions. Foremost among them are these: How does the character of Oliver withstand modern knowledge of child development? Could a child, subjected from birth to the brutalizing experiences which Oliver endures, develop into the person that Dickens presents? These considerations should make you realize that you cannot make a final judgment on the work as a whole without taking all its important aspects into account.

Another important phase of the "joint force and full result of all" is the way in which you become involved as you read. Most of what you read, if it has merit, will cause you to become emotionally involved with the characters and actions. You have perhaps observed that characters in some works seem real to you, or that incidents are described so vividly that you feel as though you had witnessed them. In these cases you were experiencing the pleasure of involvement. The problem here is whether your pleasure was fleeting and momentary ("just kicks"), or whether it has assumed more permanence (whether it resulted from a passage that is permanently, one might say spiritually, satisfying).

Your question in evaluating a work, therefore, is whether your involvement was justifiable. A work that is sentimental or melodramatic may involve you in the plights of the heroes and heroines, but when you finish it you may feel let down or betrayed, because your emotions have been expended in an obviously artificial situation. Many operatic plots suffer from this defect; considered alone they should be condemned, but no one would judge them independently of the music, because music is the ultimate cause of emotional involvement in opera.

Closely integrated with the idea of involvement is the Aristotelian theory of *purgation* or *catharsis* in tragedy. How do you regard the character of Macbeth when he kills Duncan, or of Othello when he strangles Desdemona? Shakespeare causes you to become involved with both heroes, and therefore when they perform evil deeds your own conscience cries out for them to stop. The result, when the play is over, is a "purgation" of your emotions; that is, if you experience these plays well, you will also have experienced an emotional "drain" which has been caused by your involvement with character and action. You can see that the use to which a writer puts your involvement is important in your judgment of his works.

Vitality

It may seem strange to ask if a work seems "alive" or not, but this question is valid. A good work of literature has a life of its own, and can be compared with a human being. You know that your friends are constantly changing and growing, that you learn more and more about them as your friendship progresses. A work of literature can grow in the sense that your repeated experience with it will produce insights that you did not have in your previous readings. A classic example of such a work is *Huckleberry Finn,* known to children as an exciting and funny story of adventure, but known to adults as a profound story about the growth of a human soul. Another example is *Gulliver's Travels,* in which critics for two centuries have been finding new insights and beauties. It is naturally difficult for you to predict the future, but if you have based your present opinion on reasonable grounds, and have determined that the work is good, you may conclude that within the work there will be "food for future years." In short, you may conclude that the work is vital.

Beauty

This word is another chameleon. Whole books have been devoted to an attempt to define *beauty,* and the branch of philosophy named aesthetics is concerned entirely with determining what is beautiful. Briefly, however, beauty is closely allied with unity, symmetry, harmony, and proportion. To discover the relationship of parts to whole—their logical and chronological and associational functions within the work—is to perceive beauty in a work.

In the eighteenth century there was an idea that "variety within order" constituted beauty; the extent to which Pope's couplets vary within the pattern of the neoclassic couplet is an illustration of the eighteenth-century ideal. The Romantic and post-Romantic periods held that beauty could be found only through greater freedom. This belief in freedom has produced such characteristics of modern literature as originality for its own sake, experimentation in verse and prose forms, freedom of syntax, stream-of-consciousness narration, and sometimes personal diction. Despite the apparent change of emphasis, however, the concepts of unity and proportion are still valid and applicable. Studies of style, structure, point of view, tone, and imagery are therefore all means to the goal of determining whether works are beautiful. Any one of these studies is an avenue toward evaluation. Remember, however, that an excellence in any one of them does not make a work excellent. Frequently critics use such terms as "facile" and "surface excellence" to describe what they judge to be technically correct but artistically imperfect works.

Your Preferences

Though personal likes and dislikes are the least valid criteria for judgment, they are not to be excluded. They are the principal guides to what you read, but they are valueless when purely whimsical—without any basis in thought or knowledge. They become more valuable as they reflect mature thoughts based upon knowledge. The more knowledge behind a preference, the more reliable it is, as the preference then stems not from a vacuum but from a deeply ingrained basis of comparison. The word of a well-educated adult on the value of a work is naturally more reliable than that of a child. Once you realize that your personal likes become more valuable as you learn more and grow, then these likes become more useful in evaluating literature.

You should, in writing, carefully distinguish between evaluating a work and merely liking or disliking it. You will readily admit that you might dislike works which everyone maintains are good; similarly, you may like some works that you would admit were worthless. You have heard people say "Everyone to his taste," or "I know what I like," and thus justify their preferences on unreasonable grounds. There is much truth, or course, in the argument that "personal taste is king," because preference definitely plays a part in evaluation and appreciation. But if you are to become a literate, disciplined reader, you will realize that pure subjectivism is wholly inadequate. Evaluation must be based upon more solid grounds, grounds upon which most human beings, despite personality differences, can agree.

In your themes you do not need to emphasize your likes and dislikes as a separate point, but instead your discussion should permit you to make your feelings clear by implication. The only exception occurs if you are asserting your liking despite faults, or your dislike despite excellences.

THE ORGANIZATION OF YOUR THEME

In your theme you will attempt to answer the question of whether the work you have studied is good or not. If so, why? If not, why not? The grounds for your evaluation must be artistic. Although some works may be good pieces of political argument, or successfully controversial, your business is to judge them as works of art.

Introduction

In the introduction you should briefly describe your evaluation, which will be your central idea, and you should describe the points by which you expect to demonstrate your idea. As the grounds for evaluation are many, you ought also to mention briefly those grounds which you are not going to discuss in the body of your theme.

Body

In the body you will attempt to demonstrate the grounds for your evaluation. Your principal points will be the excellences or deficiencies of the work you are evaluating. Such excellences might be qualities of style, idea, structure, character portrayal, logic, point of view, and so on. Your discussion will analyze the probability, truth, force, or power with which the work embodies these excellences.

Avoid the descent into summary or analysis for its own sake. If you are showing the excellence or deficiency of a character portrayal, you must necessarily bring in a description of the character, but remember that your discussion of the character is to be pointed toward *evaluation*, not *description*, of the work as a whole. Therefore you must select details for discussion that will illustrate whether the work is good or bad. Similarly, suppose you are evaluating a sonnet of Shakespeare, and mention that the imagery is superb. At this point you might introduce some of the imagery, but your purpose is not to analyze imagery as such; it should only be used for illustration. If you remember, as a cardinal rule, to keep your thematic purpose foremost, you should have little difficulty in making your discussion relate to your central idea.

Conclusion

The conclusion should be a statement on the total result of the work you are evaluating. Your concern here is with total impressions. This part of evaluation should underline your central idea.

Sample Theme

An Evaluation of *The Catcher in the Rye*

Despite some opinions to the contrary, *The Catcher in the Rye* is a good novel. It is written from the point of view of a deeply disturbed sixteen-year-old boy, Holden Caulfield, as though Holden were talking to us, the readers, directly. Throughout the novel this point of view is consistently maintained, and we believe in Holden as a realistic portrait of a certain type of adolescent. Technically perfect as the novel is in this respect, however, it would have only a surface beauty if it were *only* technically perfect. For this reason the degree to which Holden's character is realized, together with the strength of Salinger's vision, is most vital in an evaluation of the novel.

Though it has been a few years since I was sixteen, I believe that Holden says and does what a sixteen-year-old with his background and in his circumstances would say and do. Holden is real. A good child, he finds himself faced with circumstances with which he cannot entirely cope. Jane Gallagher is a case in point. Holden has had a pleasant and innocent relationship with her, but when he learns that Stradlater has had a date with her, he senses that she might have been seduced, even though he claims that Stradlater would not "get to first base with her." [1] As a result he wants to drive this thought out of his mind. His responses to most of what happens in the story are similarly truthful. The ducks frozen out of the Central Park lagoon and the James Castle story are therefore morbid images which cling to his mind, since they symbolize to him the harshness of life. His attempts to become harsh himself—his language spiced with profanity, his experience with Sunny —all end in unhappiness. With a capacity for dreaming, Holden finds that the world ends his dreams, or else that it provides him with dirty stuff to dream about. As a result he winds up in the hands of the "psychoanalyst guy." All his feelings are perfectly in accord with what an extremely sensitive boy would feel under these same circumstances. Salinger's portrayal of Holden is therefore "true" in the best sense.

Throughout Salinger's creation of Holden, I sense a profound pathos. Without question Salinger makes us deeply sorry for Holden's failures, and as a result we are left with little hope at the end when we learn that Holden does not know whether he is going to succeed at school. But his "little hope" makes us review the novel with an eye toward answering the question of whether the world in which Holden finds himself is really worth succeeding in on its own terms.

Here the ambiguity of Salinger's vision, and its force as he makes us strongly involved with Holden, are brought home with incredible vigor. If one only supposes that Holden is right—that children should be kept playing in the rye, and by extension be kept from becoming adults like Maurice, to name only one bad example—then *The Catcher in the Rye* is a forceful protest against our own society. The "psychoanalyst guy" wants to make Holden "mature" enough to get along, but if being mature means being able to succeed with Sunny, or to bear the vision of Stradlater corrupting Jane, then maturity is callous and society's definition of maturity is wrong. I have been told that Salinger is interested in Zen Buddhism, which is associated with the saying to the effect that "a child is a guest in the house, to be loved and respected, since he belongs to God." If this idea was in Salinger's mind when he wrote *The Catcher in the Rye*, this novel is a forceful and radical analysis of life. The idea that the child is right and the adult is wrong is fresh, invigorating, mysterious, and perhaps right.

The total effect of *The Catcher in the Rye* is that life is delicate and

---

[1] J. D. Salinger, *The Catcher in the Rye* (New York: New American Library, 1961), p. 74.

frail; since it can be so easily destroyed, it should be more carefully nourished. The author behind the idea has obviously thought deeply about life, and has done in this novel what we may expect of the best art—namely, to give a new and challenging insight into life. Right or wrong, insights of this sort cannot be ignored; nor can *The Catcher in the Rye* be ignored.

Taking Examinations on Literature

*T*AKING an examination on literature is not difficult if you prepare in the right way. Preparing means (a) studying the material assigned, studying the comments made in class by your instructor and by fellow students in discussion, and studying your own thoughts; (b) anticipating the questions by writing some of your own on the material to be tested and writing practice answers to these questions; and (c) understanding the precise function of the test in your education.

You ought to realize that the test is not designed to plague you or to hold down your grade. The grade you receive is in fact a reflection of your achievement in the course at the time the test is given. You have been admitted to a recognized institution of higher learning; therefore you may assume that you have the ability to do superior, satisfactory, or at least passing work. If your grades are low, the chances are great that you can improve them by studying in a coherent and systematic way. For many students, adequate preparation can make the difference between staying in school or leaving. Those students who can easily do satisfactory work might do superior work if they improve their method of preparation. From whatever level you begin, you can improve your achievement by improving your method of study.

Remember that your instructor prefers to see evidence of your improvement; he is anxious to read good examinations, and would like to have them all excellent. Assuming that you write literate English, your instructor therefore has two major concerns in evaluating your test: (a) to see the extent of your command over the subject material of the course ("How good is your retention?"), and (b) to see how well you are thinking and responding to the material ("How well are you educating yourself?"). Although you must never minimize the importance of factual command, the writing that reflects your understanding of these facts will be of prime significance in the determination of your grade. To phrase this idea another way: Command over facts is important, and without it your mind cannot respond properly, but once the facts are remembered, your mental sharpness assumes prominence. Ultimately, any good test is designed to elicit the extent of your understanding at that given moment, in the belief that challenging your understanding is important to the growth of your mind. There should be no cavalier disregard of factual knowledge; without a factual basis your answers, and your mind, will amount to little.

PREPARATION

With these thoughts, your problem is how to prepare yourself best to have a knowledgeable and ready mind at examination time. If you simply cram facts into your head for the examination in hopes that you will be able to adjust to whatever questions are asked, you will likely flounder, and your examination will result in a boring chore for your instructor and an unsatisfactory grade for you.

Above all, keep in mind that your preparation should begin not on the night before the exam, but as soon as the course begins. When each assignment is given, you should complete it by the date due, for you will understand your instructor's lecture only if you know the material on which he speaks. Then, about a week before the exam, you should review each assignment, preferably rereading each assignment completely. With this preparation completed, your study on the night before the exam will be fruitful, for it might be viewed as a climax of preparation, not the entire preparation itself.

Go over your notes, and as you do so, refer constantly to passages from the text that were mentioned and studied in class by your instructor. A good idea is to memorize as many significant phrases from the passages as possible; then when you are writing your exam your knowledge of a small passage can sometimes prod your memory of a long one. Also, a short quotation from the text shows your instructor that you have a good knowledge of the material. As you study, it is good to think not only about main ideas but also about technical matters, such as organization and style. Any time you have a reference in your notes (or in your memory) to technical problems, observe or recollect carefully what your instructor said about them, and about their relationship to ideas. Technique is always related to ideas, and if you show understanding of both, your exam is likely to be successful.

Your final preparation should consist of more than rereading your notes and re-examining key passages from the text. It should also contain writing and thinking, and here your ability to plan and practice your own questions and answers will be of great assistance. Make up some questions; perhaps you might rephrase a sentence from your notes into a question. Here is a brief fragment from some classroom notes on the subject of Dryden's *Absalom and Achitophel:* "A political poem—unintelligible unless one knows the politics of the time." Your sample question from this fragment might be: "Why is *Absalom and Achitophel* unintelligible without an understanding of the politics of the time?" Then you could spend fifteen or twenty minutes answering this question. Or you might look over a key passage from the text, decide what its subject is, and ask questions like "What does X say about _____ subject?" and "What is the effect of _____ in _____?" Spend as much time as possible in this way, making practice questions and answers on ideas and also on technique.

Let us try an example. Suppose you are reading Browning's "My Last Duchess." You might ask yourself this practice question about it: "Why did the Duke give orders to have his former wife killed?" Then you would begin writing an answer. About midway through you would realize that the question is difficult and ambiguous: *why* applies either to the reasons given by the Duke or to the conclusions you yourself have made. You might, as a result, recast the question into two: (1) "What reasons does the Duke reveal for having given the orders to kill his wife?" and (2) "What, in your opinion, are the reasons for which the Duke gave these orders?" You could then write a satisfactory answer to either one of these questions separately, or could also make them two parts of the original question. From this practice you would gain experience not only in asking, answering, and organizing questions, but in knowing that the phrasing of questions is important.

Your questions may, of course, be of all types. You might study the organization of a work carefully, and then ask yourself about that organization. Or you might become interested in a certain character, and wish to practice on a question asking for an analysis of that character. Time spent in this way can never be wasted, for as you carry on your practice *you are in fact studying with great care*. In addition, this practice will surely make the examination less of a surprise to you than it would be otherwise. The less you are surprised, the better will be your performance. Possibly you could even anticipate the questions your instructor might ask.

Sometimes another view can augment your own understanding of the material to be tested. If you find it possible to study with a fellow student, both of you can benefit from discussing what was said in class. In view of the necessity for steady preparation throughout a course, keep in mind that regular conversations (over coffee or some other beverage to your taste) well in advance of the examination are a good idea.

QUESTIONS

There are two types of questions that you will find on any examination about literature. Keep them in mind as you prepare. The first type is *factual,* or *mainly objective,* and the second is *general, broad,* or *mainly subjective.* In a literature course, however, very few questions are purely objective, except possibly for multiple-choice questions.

Factual Questions

MULTIPLE-CHOICE QUESTIONS   These are the most purely factual questions. You are familiar with them from college entrance exams and also, perhaps, from other courses. In a literature course, your instructor will most likely reserve them for short quizzes, usually on days when an assignment is due, to assure himself that you are keeping up with the reading. Multiple choice, of course, can test your knowledge of facts, and it also can test your ingenuity in perceiving subtleties of phrasing in certain choices. Multiple choice on a literature exam, however, is rare.

IDENTIFICATION QUESTIONS   These questions are of decidedly more interest. They test not only your factual knowledge, but also your ability to relate this knowledge to your understanding of the work assigned. This type of question will frequently be used as a check upon the depth and scope of your reading. In fact, an entire exam could be composed of only identification questions, each demanding, perhaps, five minutes to write.

What might you be asked to identify? Typical examples are:

A Character, for example, Maria in Joyce's short story "Clay." You would try to indicate her position, background, her importance in the story, and especially her significance in Joyce's design. You should always emphasize the second part, for it shows your understanding.

Incidents, which may be described as follows: "A woman refuses to go on tour with a travelling show" (assuming that either *Sister Carrie* by Dreiser or *The Big Money* by Dos Passos is being tested). After you locate the incident, try to demonstrate its *significance* in the story's main design.

Things   Your instructor may ask you to identify, say, an "overcoat" (Gogol's "Overcoat"), or "spunk water" (*Tom Sawyer*), or some other significant object.

Quotations   Theoretically, you should remember enough of the text to identify a passage taken from it, or at least to make an informed guess. Generally, you should try to locate the quotation, if you remember it, or else to describe the probable location, and to show the ways in which the quotation is typical of the work you have read, with regard to both content and style. You can often salvage much from a momentary lapse of memory by writing a reasoned and careful explanation of your guess, even if the guess is incorrect.

TECHNICAL AND ANALYTICAL QUESTIONS AND PROBLEMS   In a scale of ascending importance, the third and most difficult type of factual question is on those matters with which this book has been concerned: technique, analysis, and problems. On your test you might be asked to discuss the *structure, tone, point of view,* or *principal idea* of a work; you might be asked about a *specific problem;* you might be asked to analyze a poem that may or may not be duplicated for your benefit (if it is not duplicated, woe to the student who has not read his assignments well). Questions like these are difficult, because they usually assume that you have a fairly technical knowledge of some important terms, while they also ask you to examine the text quite rigidly within the limitations imposed by the terms.

Obviously, technical questions will occur more frequently in advanced courses than in elementary ones, and the questions will become more subtle as the courses become more advanced. Instructors of elementary courses may frequently use main idea or special problem questions, but will probably not use many of the others unless they specifically state their intentions to do so in advance, or unless technical terms have been studied in class.

Questions of this type are fairly long, perhaps with from fifteen to twenty-five minutes allowed for each. If you have two or more of these questions to write, try to space your time sensibly; do not devote eighty per cent of your time to one question, and only twenty per cent to the rest.

Basis of Judging Factual Questions

In all factual questions, literate English being assumed, your instructor is testing (1) your factual command, and (2) your quickness in relating a part to the whole. Thus, suppose that you are identifying the incident "A woman refuses to go on tour with a travelling show." You would identify Sister Carrie as the woman, and say that she is advised by her friend, Lola, to stay in New York (where the big opportunity is) and not to go on tour, where nobody important will see her. You would also try to show that the incident occurs when Carrie is just a minor dancer, during her early years in show business. But, you should, more importantly, show that her decision leaves her in New York, where a new opportunity develops, quickly enabling Carrie to become a star. You should conclude by saying that the incident therefore prepares the way for all Carrie's later successes, and shows how far she has advanced above Hurstwood's deteriorating state, monetarily speaking. The incident can therefore be seen as one of the most significant in the entire novel.

Your answers should all take this general pattern. Always try to show the *significance* of the things you are identifying. *Significance* of course works in many directions, but in a short identification question you should always try to refer to (1) major events in the book, (2) major ideas, (3) the structure of the work, and (4) in a quotation, the style. Time is short, and you must therefore be selective, but if you can set your mind toward producing answers along these lines, you will probably approach what your instructor expects.

Here are three answers that were written to an identification question. The students were asked to identify "The thing which was not," from the fourth voyage of Swift's *Gulliver's Travels*.

> *Answer 1.* This quotation serves as an example of a typical saying in the language of the Houyhnhnms. It means that the thing was false. It shows their roundabout method of saying things.
>
> *Answer 2.* This quotation is found in Chapter IV of "A Voyage to the Country of the Houyhnhnms." Gulliver is told this said quotation by his master one of the Houyhnhnms (a horse). It is brought out when the two of them are discussing their own customs and culture, and Gulliver is telling his master how he sailed over to this country. The master finds it hard to believe. He tells Gulliver that lying is altogether foreign to the culture of the Houyhnhnms. He says speech is for the purpose of being understood and he cannot comprehend lying and is unfamiliar with doubt. He goes on to say that if someone says "the thing which was not" the whole end of speech is defeated. I think what the master has said to Gulliver clearly illustrates Swift's thought that man should use language as a means to communicate truth or otherwise its purpose is defeated. We can also see Swift's thought that this very beautiful concept of language and its use is not taken up by man. This degrades mankind.
>
> *Answer 3. The thing which was not,* a variation on *"is* not," is used throughout the fourth voyage of *Gulliver* by the Houyhnhnm Master as a term for lying—telling a thing contrary to fact. The term is interesting because it shows a completely reasonable reaction (represented by that of the Houyhnhnm Master) toward a lie, with all the subtle variations upon the word we have in English. By whatever term we use, a lie is *a thing which is not* (except in the mind of the person who tells it) and destroys the chief end of speech—truthful communication. The term is therefore an integral part of Swift's attack in *Gulliver* upon the misuse of reason. A lie misleads the reason, and thereby destroys all the processes of reason (e.g., logic, science, law) by supplying it with nonexistent things. Because our civilization depends upon the reasonable pursuit of truth, a lie about anything is thus actually an attack upon civilization itself. Swift's Houyhnhnms have this value, then, that they provide us with a reasonable basis for judging elements in our own life, and hopefully, for improving them where reason can improve them.

The first answer is not satisfactory, since it is inaccurate in sentences 1 and 3, and does not indicate much thought about the meaning of the quotation. The second answer is satisfactory; despite faults of style, it shows knowledge of the conditions under which the quotation is made, and also indicates some understanding of the general meaning of the quotation. The third answer is superior, for it relates the quotation to Swift's satiric purposes in *Gulliver's Travels,* and also shows how lying actually becomes a perversion of language and reason. The distinguishing mark of the third answer is that it shows *thorough* understanding.

One thing is clear from these sample answers: really superior answers cannot be written if your thinking originates entirely at the time you are faced with the question; the more thinking and practicing you do before the exam, the better your answers will be. Obviously the writer of the third answer was not caught unprepared. You should reduce surprise on an exam to an absolute minimum.

The more extended factual questions pose, in addition to the problem of showing knowledge of facts and understanding of significance, the necessity for more thoroughly developed organization. Remember that here your knowledge of essay writing is important, for the quality of your composition will inevitably determine a part, or perhaps a major share, of your instructor's evaluation of your answers.

It is therefore best to take several minutes to gather your thoughts together before you begin to write, because a ten-minute planned answer is preferable to a twenty-five minute unplanned answer. Surprising as this idea may seem, you do not need to write down every possible fact on each particular question. Of greater significance is the use to which you put the facts you know, and the organization of your answer. When the questions are before you, use a sheet of scratch paper to jot down the facts you remember and your ideas about them in relation to the question. Then put them together, phrase a thesis sentence, and use your facts to illustrate or prove your thesis.

It is always necessary, particularly when you are dealing with "problem" questions, to work key phrases from the original questions into your thesis sentence. Let us suppose that you are given the question: "What are some reasons for which Dick Diver loses his professional abilities, and consequently drifts into oblivion?" (Fitzgerald's *Tender is the Night*). Your answer might begin in the following way: "Dick Diver loses his professional abilities for many reasons. Fitzgerald suggests that many of his energies are taken up by Nicole, but I believe that a more comprehensive reason is the paralysis of his self-esteem resulting from his superficial life among the international set . . ." Presumably, your answer would then proceed to discuss the view you attribute to Fitzgerald, and then your own. Notice that your first sentence clearly states the aims and limits of the answer, so that your answer will be completely self-contained. Whatever your method, however, do not simply start writing without reference to the question, for if your first sentence does not describe the answer to follow, your instructor will probably feel that he is reading your answer in a vacuum, and your grade will be affected accordingly. Your best approach to tests is to regard each answer as a small essay, demanding good writing, thinking, and organizing.

For comparison, here are two paragraphs from a twenty-five minute question on Fitzgerald's story "The Rich Boy." The question was: "What do Anson's two love affairs contribute to your understanding of his character?" Both paragraphs are about Anson's first love affair, with Paula Legendre:

1

The Paula affair helps understand Anson. Paula best understood him through their relationship. Anson was searching for stability and security in life; he felt he could achieve these with Paula. This was shown through the following idea: if only he could be with Paula he would be happy. Paula saw him as a mixture of solidity and self-indulgence and cynicism. She deeply loved him, but it was impossible for him to form a lasting relationship with her. The reason for this was his drinking, and his code of superiority. This was shown in the fact that he felt hopeless despair before his pride and his self-knowledge. His superiority can be further observed through his physical and emotional relationship with Paula. His entire relationship with Paula was based on his feelings that emotion was sufficient, and why should he commit himself? Her marriage greatly affected Anson; it made a cynic out of him. His attitude toward women influenced his relationship with Dolly, too.

2

To show that Anson has a dual nature, Fitzgerald develops the Paula Legendre episode at great length. Paula represents everything that Anson's reliable side needs: conservatism, equality of social and economic position, earnestness of purpose, and love. Presumably, the lengthy, low conversations between the two are presented to illustrate the positive, substantial character of Anson. But Fitzgerald is also illustrating the weakness of Anson's character—a weakness that he brings out by the relationship with Paula. As a result of a lifelong position of unchallenged wealth and status, without any real responsibility, Anson has developed into a man of shallow and superficial emotions, even though he *knows,* consciously, what mature emotions are. Thus, he cannot face the responsibility of marriage with Paula: he gets drunk and embarrasses her; he delays proposing marriage at the logical moment in the magic of love and moonlight, and therefore he lets Paula's mood vanish forever into the night. When Paula, who despite her wealth is more stable than Anson, marries another man, Anson's serious side is deeply disturbed, but his superficial side is made happy. Unfortunately, this division has made him a perpetual child, unable to cope with adult life. These same characteristics are also enforced by Fitzgerald in the affair with Dolly Karger.

It is easy to see that Column 2 is superior to Column 1. If Column 1 were judged as part of an outside-class theme, it would be a failure, but as part of a test it would probably receive a passing grade. Column 2 is clearer; it develops its point well, and uses evidence more accurately to illustrate its point.

General Questions

Many students are fond of the *general, broad,* or *freewheeling* question, which they like to regard as *subjective,* giving them the opportunity to demonstrate their mental proficiency. These students prefer the general question to the specific question, which, they feel, forces them to remember mere, picayunish details. The reason for their preference is fairly easy to assess, for frequently students may interpret a question so broadly that they ignore the obviously intended implications of the question and devote themselves to answering some other question that was never really in the instructor's mind. Then, in later discussions with their instructor, they defend their "interpretations" and plead for higher marks. Defending a poor performance in this way is deplorable and sometimes deceitful, not to speak of its damaging effect upon the purpose of education. For these reasons, many instructors avoid broad questions—and the resulting problems—entirely.

Despite abuses, however, there is a definite place for general questions, particularly on final examinations, when your instructor is interested in testing your general or "total" comprehension of the course material. You have much freedom of choice in deciding what to write, but you must constantly bear in mind that your instructor is looking for intelligence and knowledge in what you choose to say.

Considerable time is usually allowed for answering a general question, perhaps forty-five minutes or more, depending upon the scope and depth that your instructor expects. He may phrase the question in a number of ways:

1. A direct question asking about philosophy, underlying attitudes, "schools" of literature or literary movements, main ideas, characteristics of style, backgrounds, and so on. Here are some typical questions in this category: "Define and characterize Metaphysical poetry," or "Discuss the influences of science upon literature in the Restoration," or "Describe the dramatic prose of the Jacobean dramatists."

2. A "comment" question, usually based on an extensive quotation, borrowed from a critic or written by your instructor for the occasion, about a broad class of writers, or about a literary movement, or the like. Your instructor may ask you to treat this question broadly (taking in many writers) or he may ask you to apply the quotation to a specific writer.

3. A "suppose" question, such as "Suppose Rosalind were in Desdemona's place; what would she do when Othello accused her of infidelity?" or "What would Pope say about Joyce's *Ulysses?*"

Basis of Judging General or Freewheeling Questions

As these questions are fairly fluid, all the previous remarks about good writing apply. Organizing your material is a greater problem than it is on factual questions, because your choice of material is more free, and because you must solve the initial problem not only of what you *know*, but also of what to *select*. You might say that you make your own question, because your first job is to deal with general questions in terms that you can handle; you must narrow the question, but you must be sure that you stay within its limits.

Your instructor is interested in seeing: (a) the intelligence of your selection of material, (b) the quality of your organization, (c) the adequacy and intelligence of the generalizations you make about the material, and (d) the *relevance* of the facts you select for illustration.

In questions of this sort, you must avoid inconsequentiality. It is easy to write a tissue of glittering generalities which really amount to so much nonsense, unless you are careful to illustrate their truth from the assigned material. It is also easy to misinterpret the material and bring forth evidence which does not support the otherwise valid generalizations you have made. The first fault is usually a result of inadequate knowledge; the second of inadequate logic. Any low grades will reflect either or both.

PARTING ADVICE

Whenever you take an exam, use your common sense about answering questions. Answer the questions asked, and not some others, for your instructor is interested in seeing how well you follow directions and observe the wording of the questions. If the question begins "Why does . . ." be sure to explain *why* the subject indeed *does;* do not just describe *what* is *done*. If you are asked to describe the organization of a literary work, be sure to describe the *organization*. Remember that a principal cause of low grades on exams is that many students do nothing but summarize, without ever answering the questions asked. Look at the questions carefully, and answer them, trying always to deal with the issues in them. In this way, you can insure success on your exam.

B

A Note on Documentation

T IS not the intention here to present a complete discussion of documentation, but only as much as is necessary for a typical theme about literature. You will find complete discussions in most writing handbooks and guidebooks to research, and in the *MLA Style Sheet*. Whenever you have questions about documentation, always ask your instructor.

In any writing not derived purely from your own mind, you must document your facts. In writing about literature, you must base your conclusions on material in particular literary works, and must document this material. If you ever refer to secondary sources, as in themes about genre or about a literary work as it reflects its historical period, you must be especially careful to document your facts (see chapters 4 and 8). To document properly you must use illustrative material in your discussion and mention the sources for this material either in your discussion or in footnotes to it.

ILLUSTRATIVE QUOTATIONS

When you wish to make fairly extensive quotations in a theme, you should leave three blank lines between your own discourse and the quotation, single-space the quotation, and make a special indention for it. The following example is a fragment from a theme about John Gay's *Trivia,* an early eighteenth-century poem. Here is the physical layout of the writer's discussion and the quotation:

> In the poem Gay shows his familiarity with the practices of the many hoodlums and bullies of his time. According to him, many Londoners lived in dread. We may presume that they did not dare to walk the streets at night for fear of being mugged by a gang of toughs:

> Now is the time that rakes their revels keep;
> Kindlers of riot, enemies of sleep.
> His scattered pence the flying Nicker flings,
> And with the copper shower the casement rings.
> Who has not heard the Scourer's midnight fame?
> Who has not trembled at the Mohock's name?
>
> —lines 321–326

> If I thought Mohocks and Scourers would come after me to rob me and beat
> me, I would not venture out myself.

The same layout applies when you are quoting prose passages. In quoting lines of poetry, you must always remember to quote them as lines. Do not run them together. When you center the quotations as in the example, you do not need quotation marks.

If you wish to use shorter quotations, incorporate them directly into your discussion, as parts of your sentences set off by quotation marks. If you quote consecutive lines of poetry, indicate the conclusion of each line with a bar or slash (/) and begin each new line with a capital letter. Show omissions by three periods (. . .), but if your quotation is short, do not surround it with the periods. Look at the absurdity of using the three periods in a sentence like this one: "Keats asserts that '. . . a thing of beauty . . .' always gives joy." Indicate words of your own within the quotations by enclosing them in square brackets ([   ]). Here is another fragment to exemplify these practices:

> In his poem, Gay deplores the miseries of the city at night. If a person
> must go out, he discovers that "Where a dim gleam the paly [i.e., dim]
> lanthorn throws / O'er the mid pavement, heapy rubbish grows" (335–336).
> If a person is unlucky enough to go out riding in a coach, he may find him-
> self "In the wide gulf" where "the shattered coach o'erthrown / Sinks with
> the . . . steeds" (342–343).

Always duplicate your source exactly. Because most freshman anthologies and texts modernize the spelling and punctuation in works that are old, the problem may never arise. But if you use an unmodernized text, as in many advanced courses, duplicate everything exactly as you find it. Suppose that in a seventeenth-century work you encounter the word *divers* with the meaning of the modern *diverse*. If you modernize the spelling (*divers* in this sense is now archaic), you change the accent, and thereby affect the rhythm of the passage you have been reading. In prose, this change would perhaps be immaterial, but in poetry it would definitely be unfortunate. Similarly, if you start changing spelling, you should theoretically change punctuation. Or suppose you encounter a word that is no longer used; should you replace the original with a modern word with the same meaning? In other words, when do you stop modernizing and start corrupting your text? You are better off to leave it exactly as you find it.

FOOTNOTES AND INFORMAL REFERENCES

To indicate the source of all factual material you must use footnotes at the bottom of your page or at the end of your theme, or else you must, in the body of your discussion, mention the page number from the source. Though the care necessary for noting book names and page numbers often annoys many students, you should realize that footnotes and informal references exist not to cause you trouble, but to help your reader. First, your reader may want to consult your source in order to assure himself that you have not misstated any facts. Second, he may dispute your conclusions, and wish to see your source in order to arrive at his own conclusions. Third, he may become so interested in one of your points that he might wish to read more about it for his own pleasure or edification. For these reasons, you must show the source of all material that you use.

If you are using many sources in a research report, it is wise to document your paper formally. Use the formal apparatus in the section on research themes in your writing handbook or in the *MLA Style Sheet*. If you are using only a primary source, however, as is true of most of the theme assignments in this book, you may be guided by the following.

The first time you make a quotation from a source, or refer to the source, you should write a footnote, which should contain the following information in this order:

For a Book

1. The author's name, first name or initials first.
2. The name of the story or poem.
3. The name of the book, underlined.
4. The edition, if it is indicated (e.g., "Fourth edition").
5. The name or names of the editor or editors, if any. Abbreviate *editor* by *ed.,* *editors* by *eds.*
6. Within a parenthesis:
    (a) The city of publication, followed by a colon. Do not include the state or country unless the city might be confused with another (e.g., Cambridge, Mass.) or unless the city is unlikely to be known by any but natives in its particular area (e.g., Larchmont, N.Y.; Emmaeus, Pa.).
    (b) The publisher. This information is frequently not given, but it is wise to include it.
    (c) The year of publication.
7. The page number or numbers. For books commonly reprinted (like *Gulliver's Travels*) and for well-known long poems (like *Paradise Lost*) you should include chapter or part numbers or line numbers, because many readers might locate your source in a different edition.

For a Magazine Article

1. The author, first name or initials first.
2. The title of the article, in quotation marks.
3. The name of the magazine, underlined.
4. The volume number, in Roman numerals.
5. The year of publication, within a parenthesis.
6. The page number or numbers.

Sample Footnotes

[1] Joseph Conrad, *The Rescue: A Romance of the Shallows* (New York: Doubleday & Co., Inc., 1960), p. 103.

[2] George Milburn, "The Apostate," *An Approach to Literature*, 3rd ed., Cleanth Brooks, John Thibaut Purser, and Robert Penn Warren, eds. (New York: Appleton-Century-Crofts, Inc., 1952), p. 74.

[3] Carlisle Moore, "Conrad and the Novel as Ordeal," *Philological Quarterly*, XLII (1963), 59. (Notice that when you give a volume number, you do not put a *p.* before the page number.)

Suppose that in your theme you have mentioned the name of your book and the author. Then you should include only that material which pertains to publication, as in this example, assuming that John Gay's ballad opera *Polly* is the subject of your discussion:

[4] (London: William Heineman, Ltd., 1923), p. 16 (Act I, Sc. vii).

Subsequent References to Footnoted Source

For themes about one work of literature, you may use the following informal procedure. The principle of informal documentation is to incorporate as much documentation as possible into your discussion, in order to avoid the bother of footnoting.

1. In your first footnote, indicate that all later references to the source will be indicated in parentheses:

[1] Lucian, *True History and Lucius or the Ass*, trans. Paul Turner (Bloomington: Indiana University Press, 1958), p. 49. All page numbers refer to this edition.

2. The next time you refer to the source, do the following:
   (a) If you are making an indented quotation, indicate the page number, line number, or chapter number, preceded by a dash, immediately below the quotation, as follows:

> Nobody grows old there, for they all stay the age they were when they first arrived, and it never gets dark. On the other hand, it never gets really light either, and they live in a sort of perpetual twilight, such as we have just before sunrise.
>
> —p. 39

(b) If you are incorporating a quotation into your own discussion, do the following:

   i. If your sentence ends with the quotation, put the reference in a parenthesis immediately following the quotation marks and immediately before the period concluding your sentence:

> Sidney uses the example that "the Romaine lawes allowed no person to be carried to the warres but hee that was in the Souldiers role" (p. 189).

   ii. If the quotation ends near the conclusion of your sentence, put the reference in a parenthesis at the end of your sentence before the period:

> William Webbe states that poetry originated in the needs for "eyther exhortations to vertue, dehortations from vices, or the prayses of some laudable thing"; that is, in public needs (p. 248).

   iii. If the quotation ends far away from the end of your sentence, put the reference in a parenthesis immediately following the quotation mark but before your own mark of punctution:

> If we accept as a truth Thomas Lodge's statement, "Chaucer in pleasant vein can rebuke sin vncontrold" (p. 69), then satire and comedy are the most effective modes of moral persuasion in literature.

Here is a final admonition: in all cases, consult your instructor about the procedures he prefers. He is your final authority.